The Dual Economy

The Dynamics of American Industry Structure

The Dual Economy

The Dynamics of American Industry Structure

Robert T. Averitt

Smith College

New York W · W · NORTON & COMPANY · INC ·

To Tina Ruth Averitt
She persevered

Contents

Preface

THIS VOLUME attempts to deal with the world of economic experience traditionally defined by microeconomic theory. How does one go about describing a theoretical world? Is there an inevitable way or even one best way? I do not think so and the discussion in the following chapters presents no more than a possible —and I hope helpful—way to explore the structure of microeconomics.

What I have rejected is a historical arrangement of ideas or a systematically critical one that would focus on the inadequacies of traditional microtheory, especially its failure to direct present-day policy. There is an implied criticism of the old theory to be sure, but the reader will find no integrated, refined theoretical match for the rigorous logic of microtheory. My hope is that the ideas contradicting the old theory will be a starting point for seminal work. These pages represent one economist's view of a direction in which the study of American industry structure might turn. In particular, they express my conviction that the long-run problem of full-employment growth demands a new, structural microeconomics, following in general the lines pioneered by Professor Wassily W. Leontief in his input-output studies.[1]

1. Two good introductions to input-output economics are Wassily Leontief, *Input-Output Economics*, Oxford University Press, 1966; and William H. Miernyk, *The Elements of Input-Output Analysis*, Random House, Inc., 1965.

What is intended, then, is an exploratory primer of structural microeconomics, a microeconomic theory stressing the importance of the secular long run.[2] Much of contemporary, short-run–oriented microtheory is ill-suited to this purpose. Yet my intention is not to bury economic orthodoxy but to fortify it by placing it in a new perspective. Comparatively little is said about the immensely important short run because elementary micro- and macrotheories say so much, so well.

Probably because of its myopia, microtheory has contributed little to statements of recent economic policy. By 1936 John Maynard Keynes noted that the theory's practical influence was "almost destroyed."[3] With the exception of antitrust policy and the scattered use of a handful of new mathematical techniques such as linear programing, much the same is true today. The contribution of traditional microtheory to these policies is marginal; were all economists to disappear in the moment, the remaining lawyers and mathematicians could assume total responsibility for problems in these areas.

Never have the practical shortcomings of an imposing theoretical structure been more visible. For while the economics profession enjoys a spiraling prestige, the discipline's new public acclaim is almost wholly the result of the "new economics" of macroeconomic policy. The vaulting reputation of the newer macroeconomic tools—high employment surplus, fiscal drag, balanced budget multiplier—casts in bold relief the relative policy impotence of the earlier doctrine with its concepts of equilibrium price and diminishing marginal productivity. The old economics is not so much wrong as out of date.

What eroded the reputation of the neoclassical theories of competition and monopoly was the emergence and growing influence of large-scale business enterprises coupled with the demise in many industries through merger or bankruptcy of formerly numerous and relatively small firms. Even the ingenious formulation of monopolistic competition theories in the early thirties did little

2. In conventional microeconomic analysis, "long run" usually refers to a time period long enough to allow for the expansion of plant capacity, usually requiring no more than two or three years. The secular long run refers to at least a half decade, usually longer.
3. John Maynard Keynes, *The General Theory of Employment, Interest and Money,* Harcourt, Brace & World, Inc., 1936, p. vi.

to revive the sagging practical influence of microtheory.[4] By retaining the traditional assumptions of short-run profit maximization with a given plant producing a fixed group of products, these theories failed to encompass the evolution of America's industrial giants.

The manuscript benefited from critical readings by two economists, Joel Dirlam, of the University of Rhode Island, and William G. Shepherd, of the University of Michigan. Both sets of comments were invaluable. Although he did not read the manuscript in preparation, my interest in the nature of price theory owes much to my friend and teacher, H. H. Liebhafsky. Miss Kathy Messenger donated her graphic skills. My wife, Brett, was my constant intellectual companion while these ideas took shape. Having never been trained in economics, she did not share my recurrent temptation to rely on conventional analysis when the terrain was unfamiliar. If the book's central thesis still labors under a heavy burden of shopworn concepts, the fault is mine alone.

The composition of this book has been, for me, an exciting beginning to a continuing quest for a microeconomics better attuned to the structure and predicament of contemporary American capitalism. If it imparts a portion of that excitement to the reader it will have abundantly fulfilled its goal. Macroeconomics has made magnificent strides during the past generation, and we may expect more to come. Yet the most urgent theoretical challenge now facing economists lies, I am convinced, in the realm of disaggregation.

ROBERT T. AVERITT

Northampton, Massachusetts
May 1967

4. The basic works on monopolistic competition are Edward H. Chamberlin, *The Theory of Monopolistic Competition*, Harvard University Press, 1933; and Joan Robinson, *The Economics of Imperfect Competition*, Macmillan & Co., Ltd., 1933. The late Professor Chamberlin's contribution is evaluated in Robert E. Kuenne (ed.), *Monopolistic Competition Theory: Studies in Impact*, John Wiley & Sons, Inc., 1967.

The Dual Economy

The Dynamics of American Industry Structure

1. Introduction

THIS BOOK IS DESIGNED to provide the reader with a new reference for approaching a number of important economic problems.
While a few specific policy proposals are presented, particularly
in the concluding chapters, these are but samples of the policy
uses to which the analysis might be put. Most, if not all, of these
policies have been recommended by others with references outside this analytical scheme. If the reader finds my ideas useful,
he may envision policy conclusions derived from his own interests
and insights. I propose a method of approach, not a cluster of
ready-made solutions.

The argument rests upon three new concepts. By far the most
important is the distinction between center firms and periphery
firms, the two disparate types of business organization comprising
what I call the dual economy. Center firms differ from periphery
firms in terms of economic size, organizational structure, industrial location, factor endowment, time perspective, and market
concentration.

The center firm is large in economic size as measured by number of employees, total assets, and yearly sales. It tends toward
vertical integration (through ownership or informal control),
geographic dispersion (national and international), product diversification, and managerial decentralization. Center firms excel

in managerial and technical talent; their financial resources are abundant. Their cash flows are large, particularly during prosperity; their credit ratings are excellent. Center managements combine a long-run with a short-run perspective. Short-run considerations are entertained at the lower levels of the managerial hierarchy, while long-run planning is the perquisite of top management. Their markets are commonly concentrated. Taken together, center firms make up the center economy.

The periphery firm is relatively small. It is not integrated vertically, and it may be an economic satellite of a center firm or cluster of center firms. Periphery firms are less geographically dispersed, both nationally and internationally. Typically, they produce only a small line of related products. Their management is centralized, often revolving around a single individual. If located in a key industry, the periphery firm is of minor importance there. Periphery management below the top executive is, on the whole, less able than its center counterparts. Financial limitations pose a major problem to periphery firms; their cash flow is smaller, their credit rating poorer, their interest rates on borrowed funds higher than that of center firms. Their emphasis is on short-run problems, leaving little time for long-run planning. Unless they are members of the loyal opposition (discussed in Chapter 4), periphery firms usually inhabit relatively unconcentrated markets. When a periphery firm's plant capacity increases beyond some threshold level, average long-run costs *necessarily* rise.

A second departure in this book is the introduction of the firm's technical system of production as a factor in economic analysis. Firm organization and pricing behavior is significantly conditioned by the technical production mode characterizing its operations. Manufacturing is divided into three major production categories—unit and small batch, large batch and mass, and process production. The first two, generally adopted in response to the firm's market size, differ from process production that requires, in addition to a large market, a product that flows, or one produced with materials having continuous flow potential.

The third crucial concept is that of key industries. American industries are divided into a hierarchy of economic importance by using a series of loosely related criteria. Manufacturing forms the critical component of U.S. industry, and the key industries are at the heart of manufacturing. Not all of the designated key industries are central to any specific problem. The concluding chapters discuss, for example, the pivotal role of primary metals for a public policy seeking full-employment growth with a minimum of inflation. But the key industries are all "key" to one or more vital areas of economic concern.

Key industries must never be confused with center firms. An "industry" is composed of a specific commodity or group of related commodities. A key industry produces key commodities. The word "firm" refers to the business organization of an industry. Center firms quite commonly operate in key industries, but the two terms refer to different things.

A study of the dynamics of American industrial structure, its growth, technical anatomy, and business organization, this book begins with a brief history of American economic evolution, stressing the transformation of U.S. business enterprise.

2. The Development of American Business Dualism

THE EVOLUTION of the American economy from preindustrial to industrial is now completed, yet the structure of industry continues its transformation. A common form of business organization in preindustrial America was the one sketched by Adam Smith; the enterprise was run by an owner-manager who, like the contemporary barber in his own shop, worked alongside the hired help. By 1840, many American enterprises had entered the second stage that so concerned Karl Marx; the owner-entrepreneur began to devote full time to financial and managerial duties, separating himself from the workers. A capitalist class thereby emerged.

During the third organizational stage as ownership became separated from control in the largest industrial firms, a corporate form began to assert itself.[1] By severing ownership from control in the major corporations, the death of a prominent individual no longer imperiled the body corporate. No longer was a major industrial enterprise but a heartbeat away from disaster. And the national economy became insulated from the sudden demise of a critical organizing force in its key industries. By 1963 private ownership[2] had completely disappeared among the 200 largest

1. A. A. Berle, Jr. and Gardiner C. Means, *The Modern Corporation and Private Property*, The Macmillan Company, 1937.
2. Berle and Means classify a corporation as privately owned if an individual, family, or group of business associates hold 80 percent or more of the voting stock.

U.S. nonfinancial corporations. The number of management-controlled firms appearing in the top 200 corporations totaled 169, almost twice the number so controlled in 1929. Eighty-five percent of the largest 200 assets were management controlled, while only five firms (A & P, Duke Power Company, Kaiser Industries, Sun Oil, and TWA) were controlled through ownership of a majority of the voting stock.[3]

We are now moving into the fourth evolutionary stage for major corporations—the separation of the firm from the mother industry and the domestic economy. Already freed from the life cycle of human beings, large firms now seek, through conglomerate diversification,[4] to free themselves from the life-and-death cycle of specific products and even particular industries. By diversifying its product base, a large firm can imitate the structure of the American economy. A well-diversified firm tends to share in the national prosperity regardless of the fate suffered by specific products. When the U.S. economy goes slack, strong foreign markets may preserve the multinational firm's health.

The American economy's journey from a preindustrial state through the take-off into industrialism and into economic maturity wrought profound changes in the business community. Our primary concern is with these changes in business organization and production techniques during cataclysms in the economic environment. The small-firm, limited-market pattern of production that stresses a single line of technically related products dominated the economic terrain during the nineteenth century and still remains strong. In a number of industries, such as cement, bakeries, and breweries, even the more aggressive enterprises have largely confined themselves to geographic expansion, retaining their single-product orientation. But the most significant organizational outgrowth in the world of business resulting from national economic maturity was the creation and rise to ascendancy of a cluster of large-scale, multiproduct, national-international enterprises. Usually born in a fast-growing key industry, the expansionist corporation first shed its ties with its

---

3. Robert J. Larner, "Ownership and Control in the 200 Largest Nonfinancial Corporations, 1929 and 1963," *American Economic Review*, Vol. LVI, No. 4 (September, 1966), pp. 775–787.

4. A conglomerate enterprise is one that produces and sells a number of economically unrelated products. When a firm operates in many different product markets, it is not totally subject to the competitive discipline of any one market.

founding father, then its exclusive attachment to the mother industry, and is now moving across national boundaries, repudiating the last mark of parochialism—a heavy dependence on a single national economy. While a number of large firms, particularly in primary metals, have resisted this trend toward geographic dispersion and product spread, the movement in this direction among the larger business enterprises is now dominant and pervasive.

While the organization of business evolves, the techniques of production do not stand still. In the preindustrial U.S. economy, most manufacturing output was produced at the unit and small batch level. As the railroads and canals in time pried open a national market, several industrial products, including sewing machines, shoes, clocks, clothing, agricultural implements, watches, and guns moved into the large batch category. At first, the production of large batches of goods may proceed in the same labor-intensive way as in small batch times. But with the manufacturing of large quantities comes the potential for standardization of parts and moving assembly lines; in short, mass production. And the mass production of a few goods, by lowering costs and further expanding markets, leads to mass production in other sectors.

Still technical evolution has not stopped with mass production. The current industrial movement is toward process production, the utilization of materials with a potential for continuous flow. Petroleum, chemicals, and metals in continuous rolling and casting mills are prime examples of the latest stage of technical development wherein the product literally flows into the desired form or shape. Indeed, the automation of mass production extends the continuous-flow principle through the last stages of assembly and packaging. In the large-scale economy, the transformation of the business unit into a diversified, decentralized, and international organization has been accompanied by the successive removal of production labor from production. In the petty economy, where unit and small batch production still holds forth, production labor keeps, in general, its traditional place.

Contemporary American capitalism, then, is a composite of

two distinct business systems. The new economy is composed of firms large in size and influence. Its organizations are corporate and bureaucratic; its production processes are vertically integrated through ownership and control of critical raw material suppliers and product distributors; its activities are diversified into many industries, regions, and nations. Financial support is readily available from both internal and external sources. Firms in the large economy serve national and international markets, using technologically progressive systems of production and distribution. The affairs of such enterprises are conducted with a view to survival in perpetuity as they meet economic crises with successive strategies of firm expansion. We shall call this network of firms the "center."

The other economy is populated by relatively small firms. These enterprises are the ones usually dominated by a single individual or family. The firm's sales are realized in restricted markets. Profits and retained earnings are commonly below those in the center; long-term borrowing is difficult. Economic crises often result in bankruptcy or severe financial retrenchment. Techniques of production and marketing are rarely as up to date as those in the center. These firms are often, though not always, technological followers, sometimes trailing at some distance behind the industry leaders. Let us designate the firms in the small economy by the term "periphery."

The periphery economy produces useful and even indispensable goods and services; it provides employment for millions of Americans. But the center economy gives the nation its industrial might. It forms the heart of the greatest aggregation of productive potential ever known. The top 500 industrial U.S. corporations, the elite of the center economy, account for nearly three-fifths of all workers in U.S. mining and manufacturing. They participate in the innermost councils of government; they are the backbone of American industrial strength in war and peace. Without these 500, their large-scale cohorts, and their economic dependents, America would be a second-rate power. With them, she leads the world's superpowers.

Firms in the center economy act upon the assumption that they have eternal life, if not assured prosperity. Like periphery firms, they pay close attention to costs, but their future rests primarily on expanding sales. Here the first rule of survival in any but the worst times is not cut expenses, but expand sales. Expansion is bounded by the firm's ability to enter new markets, to innovate, and to sell in volume. Where prospects appear favorable, expansion can be financed with retained earnings, new stock offerings, or low-interest bank credit. The institutional guardians of American high finance gladly underwrite such sound endeavors.

The center firm is all that the periphery enterprise is not. Typically managed by one or perhaps a few hardy entrepreneurs, the periphery firm is tied to the human life cycle. When its founder dies, the business often lies mortally wounded. Usually serving a local market, periphery firm profit depends as much on cutting costs as on expanding sales. Should the market expand too much, one of the large center firms might find it worthwhile locating in the area. The periphery businessman is customarily in business to make a living, not to expand his assets. His traditional economic goal is to become a small success. In the periphery economy, a penny saved is still a penny earned.

In Chapters 5 and 6 we shall define the two economies with greater precision and analyze their economic importance. For now, we will merely assert that the economic dualism of center and periphery is well-established. It was not always so. Time was when the American economy, fragmented and rural, supported only comparatively small firms catering to local markets. Before the Civil War, corporations were a significant part of manufacturing in only one industry—cotton textiles. But as population, wealth, and cities grew, they eventually provided the environmental conditions, conducive to large business enterprise, that were further enhanced by the flow of government aid first to the canals and then to the railroads.[5]

Perhaps the most important outgrowth of railroad construction was the emergence of a new scale of economic organization. For

5. The importance of the railroads to American economic development is currently undergoing a thorough re-examination. Two outstanding recent studies are Robert W. Fogel, *Railroads and American Economic Growth*, The Johns Hopkins Press, 1964; and Albert Fishlow, *American Railroads and the Transformation of the Ante-Bellum Economy*, Harvard University Press, 1965.

the first time Americans learned how to create, organize, and sustain a mammoth commercial enterprise. Lessons learned through harsh necessity during the Civil War—how to recruit, transport, and deploy masses of men and supplies—were soon put to profitable peacetime use. By 1900, almost two-thirds of manufacturing output was produced by corporations.

By the turn of the century, several areas of the American economy began to take on a large-scale appearance. A wave of mergers ending in 1903 ensconced many of the business complexes destined to throw lengthy economic shadows. The center was assuming its contemporary form. During the 1870's virtually all American manufacturers relied upon others to supply their production factors and to market their products. By the end of the century several, producing their own supplies, sold directly to the consumer. The large, diversified, decentralized corporations molding the nucleus of our present business structure, especially in manufacturing, came significantly from two strategies of control: vertical integration with emphasis on marketing and raw material procurement, and horizontal combinations involving pools, trusts, and holding companies.

A large market provides a natural spawning site for expansive industrial enterprises, especially in industries where potential economies of large-scale operation proliferate. Such rich commercial soil could not long remain untilled. By following various combinations of four basic growth strategies giant firms soon realized a rate of growth exceeding that of the market. These strategies were expansion of volume in traditional markets, geographical dispersion, vertical integration, and product diversification.[6] Growing firms at the center of industrial activity perpetuated their lead by meeting changing circumstances with sure flexibility. The first accruing of extensive plant and personnel often came as a response to rapidly expanding demands, frequently to new demands, from technological innovations,[7] and from an urbanizing population with rising incomes. Or con-

---

6. Alfred D. Chandler, Jr., *Strategy and Structure: Chapters in the History of the Industrial Enterprise*, M. I. T. Press, 1962.
7. An innovation is the use of an idea or technique not used before. Innovations should not be confused with invention, the discovery of a new idea or technique. Inventions become economically important only when they are transformed into innovations.

versely a large enterprise may have begun through the consolidation of several small firms merged to meet a temporary crisis. To insure an outlet for a large volume of goods, distributing and marketing organizations were developed by mass-producers at the wholesale level; often, then, they moved into retailing. Having assembled the means of production and distribution, managers sought ways to maximize their use. Finally scientific management, the finishing touch to the new business syndrome, arrived.

Management, after the mechanism for assembling and combining the factors of land, labor, and capital is in operation, seeks to coordinate and perpetuate the whole endeavor. The recurring problem of corporate preservation is to overcome situations of crisis inherent in a growing, structurally changing economy. The chief functions of large-scale management, then, are two: (1) to bring together and coordinate the resources necessary for production and distribution, and (2) to institute such organizational changes required to save the firm from damage or destruction when the environment becomes unfavorable.

The first problem is essentially short run. In a going concern, top management can readily delegate detailed production decisions to lieutenants in the middle management ranks. A few well-understood rules of operation along with tight central office budgetary restraints are, in general, sufficient to insure productive efficiency when plant managers are carefully chosen and trained. Keeping a large company going requires managerial energy and talent, but such operations, once underway, quickly acquire an element of routine. Continuous production is, in part, propelled by its own momentum, freeing the managerial chiefs-of-staff for the critical long-range problem of future survival.

The economies of mass production rest heavily on the habitual repetition of specialized tasks. In the plant schedule, familiarity breeds efficiency. But rigidity and repetition, so central to the assembly line, represent the relentless enemy of the firm's long-run survival. Ever shifting patterns of technology and demand provide a hostile atmosphere for any enterprise unable to develop a set of organizational reflexes—reflexes tolerating without fail the continuing disparate threats from the outside.

Alfred Marshall, the progenitor of modern microeconomics, compares business survival to the maturation of young trees in a forest. The tender seedlings' foremost adversary is the "benumbing shade of their older rivals." Most perish, but the few which survive extend their roots deeper every day to gather increasing sustenance from the earth's minerals and moisture. It would seem, says Marshall, that the successful seedlings would grow on forever, increasing in size and strength while spreading a lengthening shadow over each new season's plucky shoots. But this is not so. "One tree will last longer in full vigor and attain a greater size than another; but sooner or later age tells on them all." [8] To Marshall, even the great corporations did not appear to be immune to the laws of the forest, for the flow of vital sap diminishes just when their future seems secure.

The forest analogy is a vivid and instructive one. Like competing trees, business firms in the same industry pose a continual threat to one another as long as each tries to expand in the home industry. No single firm can continue indefinitely to absorb more and more of an industry's output without running afoul of the antitrust laws. Thus, many of the leading firms in oligopolistic [9] industries no longer attempt to expand their share of sales in their mother markets. [THOMAS J. WATSON, JR., Chairman, IBM, commenting on IBM's having installed about 76 percent of all U.S. computer equipment—*Our market share is being reduced each year, not by an alarming amount, but it's been down for the past three years. We hope the Justice Department will be satisfied with the rate.*] [10] Nor would it be prudent to do so were the government permissive, for an enterprise that ties itself to the rhythm of a particular industry must ultimately ride to profit deterioration on the industry's life cycle. Should any firm, large or small, be so foolish as to associate itself solely with a particular mix of products, it undoubtedly must watch its profit margins dwindle near the end of the industry's rapid expansion phase when visible and sustained success attracts new capacity.

8. Alfred Marshall, *Principles of Economics,* The Macmillan Company, 8th edition, p. 315.
9. The term "oligopoly" is used to designate a market composed of few sellers. The products sold are close substitutes for one another, and market entry is usually difficult. All firms are influenced by the pricing actions of every single firm in the industry.
10. *Forbes,* Volume 98, No. 6 (September 15, 1966), p. 46.

As long as corporations act like trees, maintaining structural rigidity as they grow, how can they escape the antitruster's axe or the rot of time? Obviously they can not. And the changes which they made in order to escape such a fate radically shifts our metaphor. The American economy may now best be compared to a volatile sea with its periods of relative calm smashed by disturbances sometimes reaching hurricane proportions. Those Marshallian trees had to be hewn into sturdy corporate ships to weather the buck and toss of an economy constantly subjected to the undertow of structural change. Since Marshall wrote in 1890, floods of change, as it were, have engulfed the nineteenth-century forest drowning those institutions refusing to enter the ark of corporate flexibility.

The environment in which large center firms operate can be partially mitigated by advertising, public relations, and political pressures. The shifting moods of consumer taste can to some extent be stabilized by well-planned and executed persuasions in the mass media. But large firms must still adapt to multiple crises such as (1) downturns in the business cycle; (2) product growth lags—cycles in the demand for a single product or class of products; (3) structural changes of technological origin; (4) bottlenecks of factor supply; (5) growth in the market power of factor suppliers and buyers; (6) increased competition from imports.

Fortunately these six crisis types can be met with a single strategy: *expansion*. The four tactics of business expansion—expanding volume, geographical dispersion, vertical integration, and product diversification—when used in correct proportions and with careful timing, guarantee initial protection. The large firms in the corporate center have grown to survival size by internal expansion and corporate merger, but of the two growth forces, merger has played the critical role. Many center stalwarts merged with their competitors at the turn of the century, gaining a solid industrial underpinning before antitrust restraints became effective. With a solid economic foothold in a basic industry, they employed the techniques of merger and economic satellite formation to secure their gains. [ALFRED P. SLOAN, JR., retired Chairman, General Motors—*When I was chief executive officer of General Motors, I gave a large part of my attention to dealer relations, amounting at times, you might say, almost to a specialization. I did so because the experience of the 1920's, when the modern problems of automobile distribution took shape, taught me that stable dealer organization is a necessary condition for the progress and stability of an enterprise in this industry.*] [11]

The economic crises of the 1920's and 1930's forced vertical considerations on a wide variety of established manufacturing concerns. [JOHN D. GRAY, President, Hart, Schaffner and Marx— *Hart, Schaffner and Marx reluctantly entered the retail business in the late 1920's and during the depression years when it was forced, to avoid losing substantial sums of money, to participate in the operation of a few retail stores which had fallen far behind in payments for merchandise they had purchased from our company.*] [12]

Having established a suitable position in a basic industry and having solidified vertical relations with suppliers and distributors through ownership or satellitic control, firms in the economic center seemed secure. But after World War II most secure center firms discovered that they inhabited mature industries. Thus the third wave of mergers began in the 1950's, given an original impetus by a slackening rate of mother-industry growth and spurred on by a growing corporate pride; the notion that any good corporate management could acquire any firm in any industry and make a go of it inflated the corporate ego. Most recent mergers involve the acquisition of small firms by large ones. While many mergers combine two or more firms in the same or related industries, the late 1950's witnessed the creation of a new corporate type—the pure conglomerate. Such firms as Textron, Litton, Sperry Rand, Olin Mathieson, and Minnesota Mining and Manufacturing now range widely over the entire manufacturing spectrum, buying any enterprise that shows promise and selling those divisions that prove disappointing. The pure conglomerate is industrially eclectic.

11. Alfred P. Sloan, Jr., *My Years with General Motors*, Doubleday & Company, Inc., 1964, p. 279.
12. U.S. House of Representatives, Select Committee on Small Business, *The Impact Upon Small Business of Dual Distribution and Related Vertical Integration*, Vol. 2, 1963, p. 408.

Three great merger movements have helped to shape the American economy.[13] During the first, 1898 through 1902, the center was formed. With monopoly as its goal, the American industrial structure of the twentieth century was organized in just five years. The second merger movement, 1926 through 1930, reflected the attempts of center firms to solidify their dominance over their immediate environment by acquiring their suppliers and business customers as well as firms engaged in similar, though not identical, types of manufacture. After the first movement created horizontal clusters of enterprises similarly engaged, the second filled out the center web by providing strands of vertical control. The third merger wave, beginning shortly after World War II and continuing into the present, finds center firms seeking diversification.

There were many good reasons for center firm diversification after the war. What encouraged conglomerate merger, the marriage of industrially unrelated enterprises, can be traced to the difficulties placed in the path of traditional unions between horizontally and vertically related businesses by antitrust laws. Constricting antitrust enforcement discouraged enterprises from entering the old style horizontal merger and the later vertical ones. Center firms sought unions with firms in unrelated industries as the best means of maximizing the use of marketing and management resources.

Newly discovered products, often the accidental offsprings of company-financed research, provided further incentive for diversification. New lines developed by unpredictable research may send the progressive company into unexplored market territory. And diversification and geographical dispersion, when successfully built into the firm's managerial structure, help to cushion the blow of a recession. Since economic declines are never uniform, there are some regions that suffer less than others. During general economic declines the demand for certain products falls less rapidly than average. Revenue from relatively unaffected regions and products softens the financial impact on the firm.

Most important, diversification provides a defense against

13. Ralph L. Nelson, *Merger Movements in American Industry, 1895–1956,* Princeton University Press, 1959.

secular shifts in demand and technology. Center firms must diversify to escape the inevitable decay that Marshall predicted. But diversity in what direction? What can be used as a reasonable guide to product acquisition? The answer is found in the force that plays the dominant role in creating economic turbulence. As center firms have discovered, the root of secular disturbance in economic patterns is *technological change.*

To be safe from market erosion caused by technological change, business organizations must settle near the innovational frontiers. The outstanding characteristic of the industries into which the corporate giants have diversified during the postwar period is rapid technological change.[14] Such industries are ideal for center entry for various reasons. They form the spearhead of economic growth, allowing full rein to the expansionistic ambitions of center managers. Entry into many of these industries requires substantial amounts of capital, restricting such entry to pecunious center firms.

Since integration with factor suppliers and product distributors competes with diversification for capital funds, diversification appeals primarily to those established center firms having already achieved desired levels of integration. Finally, the key to successful diversification in the postwar period is discovered in a large number of technical personnel—a common commodity of center firms.

So it is that progressive center firms need never be left behind by a progressing economy. The more they diversify, the more they resemble the total economy. What is good for General Motors may not yet be good for the economy, but what is good for the economy is certain to benefit a flexible, diversified G.M.[15] Future shifts in the technological stream will find the center a tributary, for as technological innovation goes, so goes

14. Michael Gort, *Diversification and Integration in American Industry,* Princeton University Press, 1962.

15. Although General Motors is far from the most highly diversified U.S. firm, G.M.'s Frigidaire Division makes electric refrigerators, food freezers, automatic clothes dryers and washers, and air conditioners; Delco Appliance is a major producer of automatic oil and gas-fired residential heating equipment, while the Allison Division is a major manufacturer of turboprop engines and propellers for aircraft. G.M. is a leading producer of diesel engines. The Euclid Division produces earth-moving equipment. In addition, G.M. shares ownership of the Ethel Corporation, makers of chemical compounds used in motor fuels, with Standard Oil of New Jersey. For a good description of G.M.'s pioneering efforts to create a decentralized, multidivisional administrative structure suitable to its vast operations, see Alfred D. Chandler, *Strategy and Structure,* M. I. T. Press, 1962, Chapter III.

the center. Tomorrow's important innovations will likely flow through today's corporate channels, even when they originate elsewhere. Where technology leads, the center must follow, thus preserving itself from the twentieth century's most potent firm killer.

The research and development departments of center firms are not major sources of new invention. Individuals working alone or within the confines of small firms or universities remain the most important source of new discoveries. Indeed, center firms often lag behind their smaller rivals in the introduction of major innovations. But the superior financial and production capabilities of enterprises in the large-scale center commonly allow them to adopt quickly their own version of the new product. Massive advertising and well-established lines of distribution are usually sufficient to turn center firms into major competitors in the new market. And a merger with the original innovator can often be accomplished when the pioneering firm is small.

These nonclassical and seemingly amorphous center firms, shaped by the crises of the past, are organic. Each form contains its own evolution. Indeed, center firms literally transcend the fiction of the "corporate individual" with their perpetual life span. They present a spongy target to possible attacks by environmental enemies. Their strongest protection against future threats comes from having successfully met past threats. When the demand for a major commodity falters, center firms can concentrate their energies on other products while experimenting with new lines. When a new technology portends revolutionary potential for home industries, center firms use their financial and technical resources to embrace it. If raw material prices begin to rise, center firms can integrate backward, the antitrust division of the Justice Department permitting, and supply themselves. Where rising labor costs pose a substantial threat, automation, cybernation, or self-service may provide long-run relief, depending on the industry. Expensive production labor must now contend with easily financed capital substitution in industries where center firms dwell.

Over the years, the large firms in the economic center have developed, through successive refinements in managerial technique, corporate organizations capable of meeting any foreseeable external crisis save a major change in the rules of the economic game. Internal failures, involving breakdowns in managerial efficiency and morale, occur from time to time, but they affect only individual firms, not the center proper. It is still possible in the postwar American economy for laggard center firms to slip several notches down the status ladder. The largest 100 industrial firms in terms of assets in 1947 saw eighteen of their fellows replaced with newcomers by 1962, a third of the new entrants crashing the upper circle by way of defense contracts. But the new members of the center elite were not totally unfamiliar; all but three were among the largest 200 in 1947.[16] Nor do those who fall from the top 100 fall far. Of the sixteen dropouts that were not merged by 1963, all placed among the top 25 percent of the largest 500 industrial corporations ranked by sales volume. During the postwar era, a few center firms lost, while a few gained, significant corporate prestige in the higher corporate reaches, but center firm death has been effectively banished. A few large firms, for example, Studebaker, are forced out of their primary domestic market. Others merge with still larger concerns, giving up a separate business existence. *But no large firm simply disappears.* A study of the 1,001 largest manufacturing companies operating on January 1, 1951, showed that, when mergers were excluded, 99 percent were still in operation on September 15, 1959.[17] The decade of the 1950's did nothing to thin their ranks.

The center is faced with only three kinds of unmanageable crises: (1) major antagonistic moves by the Federal government; for instance, antitrust action against size itself; (2) major upheavals in the goals of organized labor, such as substantial profit sharing or worker's councils (to be successful, such changes would surely have to carry the weight of Federal endorsement); (3) a major shift in the trade policies of foreign nations destroying or substantially weakening foreign markets, as, for instance, the spread of Communism to large areas of the non-Communist world. Small wonder the leaders of the American business com-

---

16. U.S. Senate, Committee on the Judiciary, *Economic Concentration, Part I, Overall and Conglomerate Aspects*, 1964, pp. 208–210.

17. Frank J. Kottke, "Mergers of Large Manufacturing Companies, 1951 to 1959," *Review of Economics and Statistics*, Vol. XLI (November, 1959), pp. 431–432.

munity express continuing concern over Federal restrictions, irresponsible elements in organized labor, and Communism.

Our argument comes to this. There are two American private economies, not one. We have named one economy, the center; the other, the periphery. Firms in the center economy are large, corporate, major producers in their home industries and dabblers in others, organizing forces in their raw material markets and among their distributors. Like biological organisms their strongest instinct is to survive. They are the products of capitalism and like the system that created them, they must expand lest they contract. And by expanding their assets and diversifying their activities, they blend into the economy that contains them. So long as the general economy prospers, they prosper. So long as the economy grows, they grow.

The growth of the center in search of survival has transformed the business of America into corporate business, and even now it continues to do so at a slow but relentless pace. In 1929, slightly more than half (51.5 percent) of the working population engaged in private, nonagricultural business were employed by corporations. By 1947 the figure had risen to 55.9 percent; by 1960, to 59.7 percent. During the last generation almost 10 percent of business employment shifted from noncorporate to corporate enterprises. As with employment, so with income. Active corporations made up only 6.8 percent of the business population in 1947, but they accounted for 68.8 percent of business receipts. By 1961 active corporations had grown to 10.5 percent of total business firms, accounting for 77.1 percent of business receipts. One firm in ten is a corporation, but this tenth garners over three-fourths of business receipts.

The act of incorporation does not, of course, transform a small firm into an industrial giant. Most corporations are small, some are smaller than their noncorporate counterparts. But our figures take on added meaning when we realize that a comparative handful of corporations dominate corporate activity. This is particularly true in manufacturing, the home base of the center economy. In 1962 the twenty largest manufacturing corporations held 25 percent of the total assets of all U.S. manufacturing companies, approximately the same percentage of total assets controlled by the 419,000 smallest manufacturing firms. In addition, the fifty largest corporations held 35.7 percent of the total, the 100 largest 46.1 percent, the 200 largest 55.9 percent, and the 1,000 largest 74.8 percent. Among the 180,000 corporations in American manufacturing, 1,000 large firms controlled almost three-fourths of the total assets. Furthermore, the largest corporations earned most of the 1962 profit. The approximately 2,041 corporations with assets of $10,000 or more earned 89.3 percent of all corporate profits whereas the 178,000 remaining corporations earned but 10.7 percent of the total.

That corporate assets and profits are unevenly distributed is well known. The same is true of every highly developed private enterprise economy. Probably less well known, although more significant, is the rate of growth attained by the largest center firms. During the twelve years between 1950 and 1962 total assets of all manufacturing enterprises increased by 106 percent; those of the largest 200 manufacturing concerns climbed by 141.3 percent. Some of this rapid growth at the top came from expansion in traditional markets, but most was gained through merger with other, smaller companies. Between 1950 and 1961, the 500 largest industrials acquired 3,404 firms—an average of seven each. The top 200 corporations absorbed 1,943 firms—averaging almost ten per company. Nor were all of these acquisitions small businesses. Since December 31, 1950, over one in five of the largest 1,000 manufacturing corporations has disappeared through merger or acquisition. Between 1948 and 1963, merger or acquisition terminated the corporate life of 591 manufacturing and mining corporations with assets of $10 million or more. Had these large firms not been swallowed by fellow giants, and had they retained their size, there would have been 26 percent more firms in the over $10 million assets class in 1963.[18]

The increase in center firm diversification is clearly reflected in recent statistics. Between 1954 and 1958 the number of multi-industry companies increased by 59 percent. Such firms comprised only 1.3 percent of all companies in 1958, but they employed 44.4 percent of all company employees. In manufacturing, multi-industry companies formed 2.6 percent of the total population, but this diversified fraction accounted for 59.4 percent of company employment. The number of companies operating in more than

18. U.S. Senate, *op. cit.*, pp. 113–128.

one industry climbed by 40 percent between 1954 and 1958.[19] Diversification by merger promises several advantages to the expanding firm. It provides an established management team familiar with the field; it allows entry under the auspices of an established competitor; and it introduces the financial advantages of the large firm into a new market. Another merger motive comes, undoubtedly, from rising postwar corporate liquidity, as suggested by this candid testimony:

> The more I see of this operation the less reason I see for our buying it. But we bought it and we'll make it go. I really think it was just a matter of our company generating so much in the way of internal funds that we had to do something.[20]

It is difficult to trace the birth, growth, and spreading influence of the center economy without resurrecting American fears of monopoly power. Clearly an economy in which the three largest manufacturing corporations had combined 1963 sales of about $36 billion (an amount larger, after necessary price adjustments, than the combined sales of the 204,750 manufacturing establishments existing in 1899) represents a decisive turning away from the economic diffusion of nineteenth-century America.

That American manufacturing emerged from the nineteenth century highly concentrated cannot be denied. A thorough study in the late 1950's by Professors Kaysen and Turner consolidated manufacturing industries into 147 categories.[21] They found fifty-eight of these highly concentrated (the eight largest firms accounting for half or more of sales, the twenty largest making 75 percent or more), while another forty-six industries qualified as simply concentrated (the top eight firms sharing at least a third of industry sales, the leading twenty less than 75 percent). But economic concentration within specific markets is now of long standing, and is probably increasing very slowly if at all. Any company consistently expanding its share of a particular market is certain to attract the attention of the increasingly

19. Joel B. Dirlam, "Recent Developments in the Anti-Merger Policy: A Diversity of Standards," *The Anti-trust Bulletin*, Vol. IX (1954), pp. 412–413.
20. John R. Bunting, *The Hidden Face of Free Enterprise*, McGraw-Hill, 1964, p. 37.
21. Carl Kaysen and Donald F. Turner, *Antitrust Policy: An Economic and Legal Analysis*, Harvard University Press, 1959.

effective antitrust division. Even as center firms have expanded their influence in the total economy, the erosion of local and regional monopolies, often enjoyed by relatively small firms, and the growth of consumer incomes, shifting the pattern of consumption away from manufactured products toward services where concentration is least evident, have held the over-all level of monopoly roughly constant.

Other fears concerning concentration may also be assuaged. Most economists admit that large corporations possess substantial private taxing power implied by their ability to administer prices within a reasonable range. In addition, their ability to issue new stock, a highly liquid asset, resembles the government's function of coining money. Yet it may be that large firms make useful and even necessary expenditures with their private tax revenues that would be impossible if left to consumer consent. Would more competitive levels of profit allow current expenditures on private research and product development? The rapid rate of automation now in progress could fail to command a majority if forced to stand a popular vote, but these highly disruptive changes may provide the essential productivity of the future.

Our purpose is neither to defend nor decry big business. We propose, rather, an examination of the possible social uses of industrial concentration, coupled with an evaluation of its social liabilities. We shall discover that the potential social benefits of the center economy are considerable once its nature and position in the American economic structure are understood. The next several chapters are devoted to the development of that understanding.

3. The Technical Anatomy of the U.S. Industrial System

MEN WHO DEVOTE THEIR CAREERS to business in America are profoundly persuaded of the system's complexity. Those who experience the inner workings of business enterprise stand ready to assure the outsider that no two businesses are alike. Every firm has its own corporate style, its unique position in the market, its individual network of communication, production, and distribution. No academic stereotype or abstract model, we are warned, can do justice to the multiplicity of American commerce and industry. To those who meet the payroll, the pitfalls of generalization are exceedingly clear.

Yet generalize the economist must if he is to ply his trade. From the welter of diversity the skillful economist plucks the common threads that weave patterns of individuality into a business system or systems. Considering only manufacturing and distribution, what common bond unites the steel mill and the textile mill, the toy shop and the machine shop? Do the baker and the candlestick maker have enough in common to justify a general theory of "the firm"? Economists assure us that they do share common procedures on two levels—the fiscal and the physical. On the fiscal level, all businesses contract *costs* and earn *revenues*. The major task of elementary supply theory is to define the relationship between costs (marginal and average, variable and fixed) and revenues (marginal and average) as the firm's output varies. The characteristic physical function of all firms is to secure *inputs* (land, labor, capital, and management) and convert them into a saleable *output* (a product or commodity).

Two paired concepts, then, are essential—costs and revenues, inputs and outputs. By discovering the absolute magnitudes, direction of change, and rate of change of these abstractions, the microtheorist builds a useful model for understanding an economy appearing at first too complex for human comprehension. It is an invaluable theoretical construction, the theory of the firm, combining beauty and learning, rigor and simplicity. To those who trouble to master its technical terms it offers the thrill of insight and the prestige of erudition. Yet from time to time the accepted theory of the firm gives rise to a recurring sense of omission. Surely theory must simplify and deal abstractly with experience, but must the gap between firm theory and observed business practice be so great? Can a description of business behavior that shows the practical man of business so little that is familiar be complete?

The purpose of this section is to build a bridge between the "firm" of the economist and the technical system of production as it exists in American manufacturing. Our central idea is that the organization and behavior of manufacturing enterprise, center and periphery, are significantly conditioned by the technical production type characterizing the firm's operations.

Unit and Small Batch Production

WE SHALL BEGIN with the earliest type of manufacturing technique. Unit and small batch production is at the same time a very old and a very new type of production. As Adam Smith observed almost two hundred years ago, small batch production prevails where the market is severely limited. We must now add that it hangs on tenaciously where styling is critical and where technological change is exceedingly rapid. Unit and small batch production includes (1) production of units to customer's requirements (large electrical generating equipment), (2) production of prototypes (experimental aircraft and automobiles), (3) fabrication of large equipment in stages (major missile systems), and (4) production of small batches to customer's orders (dies from the machine tool industry). It is the characteristic production type in such diverse industries as custom clothing and furniture, heavy electrical equipment, the aerospace industry, and the machine tool industry. Although now decreased in relative importance, it seems likely to persist so long as large items of equipment have to be fabricated, where technical development proceeds rapidly enough to make standardization impractical, and where individual idiosyncrasies of demand are important.

Unit and small batch production is predominantly craft oriented. The older industries depend on the traditional crafts, for example, clothing design, material cutting, and tool and die making, while the newer, technically dynamic industries depend on the professional craftsmen in engineering, physics, and chemistry. The craftsmen, traditional and professional, are pivotal in unit and small batch production. Their efficiency and productivity determine the efficiency and productivity of the entire plant. As their work goes, so goes the enterprise, or at least that part of the enterprise specializing in unit and small batch output. The proportion of skilled production workers is relatively large.

Production schedules in unit and small batch plants are based on orders received. Thus planning can only be very short term. *Development* is the most critical function of the firm, making manufacturing operations difficult for management to control. With so much time and money spent in developing the product, any attempt to tighten production schedules will likely achieve little speed-up and may create considerable bad feelings among technicians. The work progresses at the pace set by the craftsmen, and they set their own rhythm. Communication between production and development personnel is usually informal and intimate; production problems must be solved by development people. Salesmen must also be knowledgeable about the techniques of production and design, for they sell *ideas* and *technical potential,* not a finished product.

The advantage of unit and small batch production—flexibility

—implies an extravagant use of facilities and less than maximum efficiency in most operations. The cost per unit is inevitably high. Prices tend to be flexible, based on what the market will bear. When unit and small batch production firms are small but sell to large enterprises, prices tend to be forced down toward the range of opportunity costs.[1]

Large Batch and Mass Production

As THE MARKET expands, production rises into a new category— large batch and mass production. Heavy mechanical and light electrical products tend to fall into this class; automobile production is the most familiar example to Americans. Some form of moving assembly line, as pioneered by the Ford Motor Company, is quite common in large batch and mass production. Management planning is relatively long-term, production schedules are not directly dependent on orders. The short-run success of the firm depends mostly on productive efficiency (reduction of costs), although long-run prosperity depends on development as well. A communications gap tends to develop between the research and production departments, and between production and marketing. The sales staff usually has scant technical knowledge, selling whatever the firm produces.

Under large batch and mass production management meets its maximum challenge. While defining the limits under which the organization must operate, the physical work flow does not determine the organizational mode as it does in unit and small batch work. The familiar line-staff type of management framework is most highly developed here; in recent years the centralized line-staff pattern has given way to a series of line-staff networks covering various products or geographic regions.[2] Formal, elaborate management systems are characteristically

1. Opportunity costs are measured by the income that a productive factor, for example, capital or labor, would receive in its most lucrative alternative employment. A price that reflects only opportunity costs is the minimum feasible long run price.
2. The management of most large enterprises is divided into line and staff functions. Line managers bear the responsibility for the firm's day-to-day operations, while staff managers coordinate the firm's activities and make decisions affecting the firm's long-run goals. While a line manager might, for instance, set prices for the products produced by his division, staff management makes decisions pertaining to the allocation of capital for new investment.

successful in maximizing large batch output while minimizing costs. Under such systems the flow of administrative paper reaches its peak. Top management's primary objective is the *survival of the firm;* production and marketing strategies commonly treat profit as little more than a tool which keeps the firm alive.

When market expansion allows an industry to move up the technical hierarchy from unit and small batch to large batch and mass production, the skilled craftsman is typically replaced by large numbers of unskilled workers. The product is standardized enabling each small part of the craftsman's job to be assumed by workers with little or no prior training. The skilled workers who remain are responsible for the maintenance of tools and plant. Unlike the traditional pattern in unit and small batch production, where the owner often begins as a craftsman, the worker and management are separated by a gulf of education and social background. The individual worker may climb the management ladder, but he usually reaches only the foreman rung.

The possible strain in relations between manager and managed is nowhere greater than in large batch and mass production; much of the industrial tension collides in the person of the foreman. No longer a worker and yet only on the fringe of management, the foreman often inhabits a no man's land in corporate society. His reputation and success depend largely on his ability to fathom the mood of management. The good foreman makes his production schedule when scheduling is stressed, cuts down his stock when inventory reduction is the key phrase, concentrates on quality control when customer complaints threaten sales. As in the Soviet economy, production goals are often met by a variety of "drives" toward one or another objective, but unlike his Russian counterpart the American foreman may find it difficult to discern the proper mix of current managerial concerns. The U.S. business system enjoys considerable goal flexibility, but it does so to the detriment of the foreman's nervous system.

Manufacturing firms characterized by large batch and mass production lean toward cost-plus or "break-even point" pricing, with a preference for sticky prices (administered prices), particularly immobile in a downward direction. They are, for the most part, price makers and quantity takers. They are faced with a divergence between maximum short-run and optimum long-run revenue. Maximizing short-run revenue is likely not to pay in the long-run race for survival. Frequent price cuts should be avoided because (1) they disturb production planning; (2) they may bring in few new customers while making regular customers suspicious.

Process Production

THE NEWEST production type, process production, is becoming increasingly important. Any manufacturing procedure which can be converted to continuous material flow is a candidate for process production. Originating with the manufacture of liquids, gases, and crystalline substances, it is spreading to the making of solid shapes—steel, aluminum, and engineering parts.

Absolute capital costs soar in process production, making the barriers to new firm entry substantial. But if the plant can be operated full time at near capacity levels, the per unit costs of capital can be dramatically reduced. The best plant manager in process industry is the one who can keep the plant loaded up—that is, operating near its economic capacity. High level operation can so significantly cut unit costs that process firms characteristically act in the way predicted by Professor Baumol— they maximize sales (production) subject to a profit restraint.[3] The firm's most critical function is *marketing;* low costs depend directly on high sales volume. Storage is usually difficult or impossible.

Planning in the process firm is very long term. The physical limitations of production are well known. Since the major production bottlenecks are mechanical rather than human, output targets can be effectively set and reached. The limited necessity for temperamental craftsmen removes a barrier to output increases operating in unit and small batch production.

3. William J. Baumol, *Business Behavior, Value and Growth,* Macmillian, 1959.

Process management relaxes its watchdog duty becoming less formal than large batch and mass production management. The distinction between line and staff personnel is hazy because technical specialists, exercising executive responsibility, are incorporated into the line organization. Management by a committee representing various technical talents is the norm, with committee decisions reached after an exchange of information and appraisals of technical data. Decision making is truly a joint affair with each committee member using his particular specialty to promote the firm's production and financial objectives. In large batch and mass production management committees are common enough, but there they are more political than operational. Their real function outside process production is to achieve managerial consensus rather than technical expertise.

Unskilled workers represent the minority in process industry; skilled workers, highly educated professionals, are critical. Routine work is performed by machinery, with tense, taxing work occurring only during infrequent machinery failures. During crisis breakdowns the workers willingly toil with a spirit of cooperation, repairing the damage so that production can be resumed. Morale is usually high, personnel relations comparatively easy.

Most technical decisions, including those during crisis, must be delegated by top management for technical reasons. Policy decisions extend beyond one man's responsibility. The chief executive is free of production matters and much of the burden of planning. He becomes the pivotal figure in the firm's social organization, a figure surrounded by ritual—he performs industrial and public relations ceremonies daily.

Any attempt to divide American manufacturing techniques into three hard-and-fast categories involves oversimplification. It is difficult, for instance, to make a sharp quantitative break between small batch and large batch production. But although the dividing line is blurred, our classification of production categories charts business behavior fairly well. The U.S. economy's historical progression has clearly been from unit and small batch toward large batch and mass production as scattered geographic markets merged and population and incomes multiplied. Inspired by the overhead trolley used by Chicago packers in dressing beef, Henry Ford employed the moving assembly line to convert large batch auto assembly into mass production. The current impetus toward automation in a variety of mass production industries is but another step upward in the productive hierarchy.

Process production represents the newest and most technically advanced stage. It is partly an outgrowth of a spreading chemicalization of production. Any product that flows, or that can be produced with materials having continuous flow potential, can be classified within process production, currently the most complex production technique offering high-speed output and low per unit cost.

Production Types and the Theory of the Firm

AN INTEGRATION of our production typology with the accepted theory of the firm is complicated by the fact that most firms combine two or more production techniques. Most chemical firm production, for instance, may be process production, but if a firm packages its product, packaging operations then fall into the large batch and mass production category. The two giants of the electrical industry, General Electric and Westinghouse, encompass unit and small batch production (heavy electrical generating equipment) as well as large batch and mass production (light electrical appliances). Many amorphous corporate concerns harbor two or more distinct universes of technical operation; efficient management demands that the corporate bureaucracy give explicit recognition to the importance of production technique. The president of Westinghouse Electric divided its diverse operations, including 73 profit centers and 107 plants, into two major sections, both averaging over $1 billion a year in sales. [DONALD C. BURNHAM, Westinghouse President — *The half in which you know your customers was put under George Wilcox. The other half I put under our best man on high-volume work—Ron Campbell. The division made sense because there's a difference between selling a turbine-generator and an electric toothbrush.*] [4]

By moving up the scale of technical complexity, American manufacturing has extended its planning horizon. Unit and small

4. *Forbes*, Vol. 95, No. 11 (June 1, 1965), p. 25.

batch output, based on orders only, conditions entrepreneurs to short-run considerations. Large batch and mass production remove output from immediate dependence on day-to-day sales, while process production is economically feasible only if a high volume outlet is assured. Hence, large batch and mass production products submit to long-term planning, while process production strongly encourages very long-run planning.

The analytical key to microeconomics, unifying the theory of supply and of demand, is price. So fundamental is pricing to supply and demand analysis that this body of doctrine has become widely known as "price theory." Yet no portion of economic doctrine shows a wider split between academic assumption and business practice. Microtheorists conventionally assume that firms maximize short-run profits; that they do so by producing that output which equates marginal cost (the cost of producing the last unit) with marginal revenue (the revenue gained from the sale of the last unit). But when three distinguished economists made a careful investigation of pricing practice in large business, they uncovered an abundance of cost-plus pricing.[5] Based on his experiences as a business consultant, Professor Baumol hypothesized that many large firms set prices to maximize sales within a minimum profit restraint.[6]

Perhaps all three theories of pricing practice—short-run profit maximization, cost-plus markups, and sales maximization within a minimum profit restraint—are correct. Our major point is that business pricing strategy for a particular product is intimately related to the product's production type. As we noted earlier, the critical activity under unit and small batch production is *development*. The output is not standardized and cannot be mass produced; where style or design is crucial to sales, the craftsmen, professional and skilled, occupy a pivotal place. Unit and small batch firms *do* tend to maximize short-run profits, charging what the market will bear as orthodox theory suggests. They equate marginal cost and marginal revenue within the lim-

5. A. D. H. Kaplan, Joel Dirlam, and Robert Lanzillotti, *Pricing in Big Business,* The Brookings Institute, 1958, p. 256; cost-plus pricing under a variety of business conditions as practiced by American oligopolists is discussed in Richard Ruggles, "The Nature of Price Flexibility and the Determinants of Relative Price Changes in the Economy," in *Business Concentration and Price Policy,* Princeton University Press, 1955.
6. *Op. cit.,* Chapters i and vi.

its of their ability. If their markets are crowded with competitors, the price is pushed down. If they are monopolists, they exhibit classic monopoly behavior. We must not forget that neoclassical theory, whence springs the current theory of the firm, was formulated when unit and small batch production characterized the productive mode in both England and the United States.

Once large batch and mass production begin to dominate industrial activity, *production* displaces development as the primary managerial concern. Here the greatest gains can often be realized, not through maximizing selling price, but through minimizing costs. The price of a Ford touring car on October 1, 1909, was $950. By December 2, 1924, the price had been reduced to $290. This dramatic reduction in price, and the new markets it opened, reflected the cost savings that resulted from mass production.

Oligopoly is the natural market structure counterpart to large batch and mass production. When a product is sold under oligopolistic conditions, any initial price decline will likely be followed by all competitors to prevent sales losses to the price cutter; price increases will *not* be followed by one's competitor unless the initiating firm is the industry price leader and other firms share a consensus favoring the increase. Administered prices soon become the rule, with the prevailing price commonly set to insure the *survival* of all reasonably efficient firms. The pattern is one of price leadership initiated within an informal industry consensus. One might argue that survival pricing maximizes very long-run profit during the lifetime of participating firms, but it does not result in the necessary equation of short-run marginal cost and revenue.

In process production, *marketing* is paramount. Unit costs will automatically fall until existing plants are operated quite near their engineering capacity. Here prices may be flexible on the down side or, more likely, firms will engage in heavy advertising expenditures in affluent economies to create and sustain a viable demand for their product. The primary objective of process firms is to stimulate long-run increases in demand while maintaining short-run gains. Price discounts to foster market encroachment on substitute products is a useful strategy when the buyers are other business firms; advertising is often more useful when the product is sold under a trade name to the public.

In summary, firms based on unit and small batch production are short-run oriented, typically short-run profit maximizers as assumed by conventional theory. If capital barriers to entry remain insignificant, craftsmen can set up their own shop and become their own boss. When such firms become numerous in a single market, they approximate the model of perfect competition; when a single firm holds the field, it approaches the behavior described by monopoly theory.

Firms specializing in large batch and mass production, or the operating divisions of firms with such a specialty, have a longer run perspective; they compete in cost reductions and sales increases (largely through advertising) while maintaining relative price stability. If the dominant firm in the industry is large enough to attract antitrust attention, it may turn its aggressive sales attentions to other products in other industries. When the industry consensus is permissive, price changes are often, but not always, announced by the dominant firm. Pricing is set to insure efficient firm survival, not to maximize short-run profits. A form of cost-plus pricing is employed, using a general "average industry" cost as a guide.

Process product pricing generally follows the strategy of maximizing sales with a profit restraint. Oligopoly is again the dominant market structure, leading to competition in cost reduction and advertising where product sales are likely to respond to advertising. There is usually heavy emphasis on distribution; often industry technology is stressed ("Better Things for Better Living through Chemistry"). Prices often fall, particularly when an item is moving from product status (a relatively new innovation) to that of a commodity (a well-established and widely imitated item). At times products can be saved from the commodity heap through small changes. [Vice-President ARTHUR W. LUCAS, Monsanto Chemical — *If a product lends itself to innovation, you can prolong its maturity, and this keeps it from becoming a commodity.*] [7]

Prices are not, of course, even under strict oligopoly, deter-

7. *Forbes,* Vol. 96, No. 2 (July 15, 1965), p. 20.

mined merely by the industry's dominant technique of production. What we are suggesting is that the technical production type is one of the many forces, including, for example, a desire to bar industry entry and to stimulate long-run increases in demand, operating on price setters. But as one determining force, the technique of production is omnipresent in every industry, sometimes central to pricing decisions while at other times submerged.

Process production is the optimum type for consumers as a group unless a single firm or a few firms acting as a single unit are able to prevent imitators. [WILBUR G. MALCOLM, Chairman, American Cyanamid Company — *What you're after is to get into product lines that you yourself control, either through patents or trademarks.*][8] When products are not shielded from competition, process firms experience downward price incentives *or* upward advertising cost incentives or both. Assuming that the advertising is presented to consumers in an appealing way or that it helps finance consumer entertainment, either alternative yields some consumer benefit. Some high initial profit on new innovations will probably secure internal funds for additional research, although undoubtedly much of this expenditure will go into firm "insurance," most often defensive research on products other firms are suspected to be developing. Such self-defense makes process firms appear more inventive than they are in fact.

We must conclude this section with a word of caution. We have grouped large batch and mass production together because the production of large quantities of merchandise has historically resulted in standardization and reductions in unit costs. When demand grows, the traditional small batch techniques are not simply expanded, but in time become obsolete, and a totally new concept of production is inaugurated. When the product is liquid or has liquid properties, as, for example, petroleum, most chemicals, steel, aluminum, and most plastics, we have called the new productive techniques "process production." When the product cannot be handled in liquid form, but can be made to flow by means of assembly lines or other locomotive techniques, we have labeled the productive mode "mass production."

8. *Forbes*, Vol. 93, No. 12 (June 15, 1964), p. 23.

The distinction, then, between mass and process production is somewhat artificial. Both depend on product flow and on very large markets. Overhead costs are considerable in both cases. But discrimination between the two production modes is useful in pointing up the shift in emphasis from *production* costs to *marketing* costs, and from *formal* managerial systems to *informal* ones. The earliest form of mass production, typified by meat packing and auto production, necessitated large quantities of low-skilled labor. Worker time and motion, the speed of the line, become a critical cost consideration. Since human beings must be speeded up to cut costs, formal managerial arrangements are useful. Close managerial supervision of the human element in production pays handsome cost economies.

When the product can be made to flow, the need for low-skill labor is greatly reduced; production is much more automatic, and cost reductions depend more heavily on plant load—another name for sales. Thus mass production firms have not neglected marketing, for they are dependent on a mass market, but they most closely attend to production. As old-style mass production techniques become automated, removing low-skill labor from the line, mass production management shifts its attention to marketing. Automation blurs the original distinction between mass and process production.

The historic thrust of manufacturing, then, is away from unit and small batch production into old-style mass production, then onward to continuous-flow output. The corresponding managerial evolution turns from rigid bureaucracy toward a concentration on marketing. To be sure, the shift is one of *emphasis;* production will always be important to all firms. But continuous flow techniques are more automatic, and they automatically reduce unit costs when output rises toward engineering capacity in response to rising sales. [ARCHIE E. ALBRIGHT, Executive Vice-President, Stauffer Chemical Co. — *As long as big, efficient plants are run at high levels of capacity, it is possible to make satisfactory profits even on bulk-type chemicals.*][9] The long-term technical trend in American manufacturing moves toward lower prices, or price stability under rising demand and rising selling costs. At the

9. *Forbes*, Vol. 98, No. 10 (November 15, 1966), p. 42.

consumer level, the two tendencies often cancel one another out. A few industries, like basic steel, may resist for a time the movement from large batch to continuous flow, but soon or late, when technically feasible, the shift begins, bringing with it more intense price and selling pressures. Big-volume continuous casting steel machinery is being installed by the U.S. Steel Corp. and National Steel.[10]

In the basic steel industry, the conversion from large batch to process production (continuous rolling and casting mills) is limited by the instability of demand. Although continuous rolling production drastically cuts unit costs when the plant is loaded up, idle plant time is extremely expensive. Any steel capacity periodically forced into standby status may have to retain the large batch technology. Should the government initiate and maintain perpetual full employment in the near future, a beneficial side effect would be the growing economic feasibility of lower cost continuous production facilities in industries like steel and aluminum.

The Hierarchy of American Industry Structure

WE HAVE COMPLETED our first excursion into the technical anatomy of the U.S. industrial system. Exploring the network of existing production types, we divided them into three categories—unit and small batch production, large batch and mass production, and process production. Yet another aspect of the technical economic structure looms before us, for the body economic, like the human body, is a composite of intertwined and coordinated parts. If our three production types compose the economic bone structure, we must now plot the circulatory network of American industry.

Every modern industrial structure can be divided into sectors. The simplest sectoral breakdown is into three broad groups—agriculture, industry, and services. A more extensive, and more useful, scheme of classification might divide the economy into mining, construction, manufacturing, transportation and communication, trade, finance, and government. Should we need a

10. *Business Week,* No. 1,945 (December 10, 1966), pp. 176–182.

still more intricate delineation, these major sectors can be subdivided.

All sectors in the American economy are important, but some are more important to industrialization than others. We recognize this when we use the terms "key industries" or "basic industries." Our first insight into the hierarchy of industry importance comes with the answer to this question: Which industries perform especially critical functions in the economy?

Our first reaction may be to reject such a question. In one sense, each of the major functions performed in any modern industrial complex is necessary. Agriculture, mining, manufacturing, trade—all of these must be offered domestically or else imported, for they support one another. An overriding fact about any industrial economy is its close structural interdependence. But perhaps the term "industrial" provides a clue. The activity most often missing or severely undernourished in the economies of nonindustrial countries is manufacturing. Wholesaling, retailing, construction, agriculture, mining—these are major identifiable activities in underdeveloped regions, though they may be but primitively performed. The American economy, then, is a developed economy because it relies heavily on manufacturing for its income and employment. Indeed, the rise of domestic manufacturing, along with modern services, is often considered as synonymous with economic development.

There is one apparent exception to this generalization, and we must recognize it before going on. Those activities commonly grouped under the title "social overhead capital" are traditionally underdeveloped in poor countries, but they are not located in the manufacturing sector. Under a narrow definition, social overhead capital includes transportation, communication, power, and water supply. The term is sometimes used to include all public services from law and order through education and public health. Social overhead capital industries share the following characteristics. (1) They substantially facilitate the engendering of a large variety of other economic activities, particularly manufacturing. (2) The organizations providing social overhead capital services are usually publicly owned or regulated; often called public utilities, they are for the most part privately owned but regulated in this country while often owned by the public in other parts of the developed world. Decades of debate notwithstanding, the difference in performance is not great, other factors being equal. (3) The services cannot be imported.

Using the narrow definition of social overhead capital—transportation, communication, power, and water supply—we find that these facilities are important for economic growth primarily because they provide the necessary preconditions for the expansion of other industries, especially manufacturing. Thus social overhead capital does not really constitute an exception to the singular importance of manufacturing in creating a self-sufficient, industrial economy. Since their significance rests so heavily on this relation to manufacturing, and since their policies are so closely circumscribed by government, we will confine our attention to other sectors.

Size alone imputes critical importance to the manufacturing sector in the United States. American manufacturing accounts for almost one-third of total output, employs one-fourth of all workers, and pays one-half of all corporate income taxes. Within manufacturing, American national affluence assures that those industries having significant economies of scale will loom large. Studying fifty-one countries including the United States, Hollis B. Chenery found that "industries having significant scale effects produce about 40 per cent of manufacturing output at an income level of $300 and 57 per cent at $600." The large U.S. population contributes to the same result. "An increase in population from 2 to 50 million causes manufacturing output per capita to nearly double and the sectors having significant economies of scale to more than triple." [11] As population and income increase in an economy, the manufacturing sector assumes a magnified importance. And within manufacturing, industries characterized by significant scale economies assume ever-increasing ascendancy.

11. Hollis B. Chenery, "Patterns of Industrial Growth," *American Economic Review,* Vol. L (1960), p. 645.

Key Manufacturing Industries

THE ISOLATION of manufacturing narrows our search for the industrial nucleus considerably. In 1963 there were 4,797,000 business firms in operation, but only 313,000 of these were in manufacturing. Yet manufacturing is an exceedingly broad term, covering activities of considerable diversity. How can we isolate the most important sectors within manufacturing? Can we set forth a series of criteria in addition to the nebulous "economies of scale" suggested by Professor Chenery? No such set of criteria can hope to gain universal acceptance, perhaps none can muster a professional consensus. Yet the term "key" or "basic" industries continually recurs in the writings of economists, indicating a recognition that some grounds exist for separating the more important industries from the industrial mass. The following eight guideposts to importance, taken together, seem to offer a reliable index to the industries composing the heart of American manufacturing.

1) TECHNOLOGICAL CONVERGENCE: Industrialization in nineteenth-century America was characterized by the spreading adaptation of metal-using technology employing decentralized power sources. Throughout the expanding machinery and metal-using sectors there arose a technological convergence. Metal-cutting machinery requires a small number of operations—turning, boring, drilling, milling, planing, grinding, polishing—which pose common problems of power transmission (gearing, belting, shafting), control devices, feed mechanisms, and friction reduction.

During the nineteenth century, prior to the development of the current patterns of vertical integration, individual production sequences leading to the final product were characteristically undertaken as separate operations performed by independent business firms. With poor interchange among firms, the spread of advanced techniques was dependent on a catalyst for the dissemination of the rapidly advancing industrial know-how. The machine tool industry provided just such a cluster of information centers. Dealing with processes and problems common to many industries, the machine tool industry constituted a pool of skills and technical knowledge employed throughout the manufacturing sector of the economy.[12]

After World War II, the industrial catalytic function shifted from machine tools to the chemical and electronics industries. Indeed, automation, the destabilizing infant of electronics, began during the postwar period to transform the production and design of machine tools. Computers and electronic data-processing equipment now register a revolutionary influence along a broad industrial spectrum, filling a role similar to that played by machine tools in an earlier era. The chemical industry has also broken through traditional industry bounds. Synthetics have replaced natural fibers, rubber, soaps, and fertilizers. The chemicalization of the industrial process is threatening to erode the raw material base on which the industrial revolution rested; DuPont's Delrin and the Celanese Corporation's Celcon are beginning to replace die-cast zinc, brass, aluminum, and steel in automotive parts, instrument panels, appliances, pipes, and plumbing. Lexan from General Electric can be drawn, stamped, and cold-formed as easily as low-carbon steel. [JOHN O. LOGAN, retired Executive Vice-President, Olin Mathieson Corp. — *These days everything is chemical. Even the steel industry is just a specialized branch of chemistry.*] [13]

Technological convergence industries, then, are three: the historically dominant machine tool industry and the newly important chemical and electronics industries.

2) CAPITAL GOODS: All economists recognize the special significance of the capital goods industries. They are critical for both economic growth and economic stability.

Studying the structure of the United States economy for the year 1939, Robert Grosse divided economic activity into 68 industries.[14] Using this classification, Grosse found that 75 percent of the capital stock was produced by only four industries—construction, transportation equipment, electrical equipment, and

12. Nathan Rosenberg, "Technological Change in the Machine Tool Industry, 1840–1910," *Journal of Economic History*, Vol. XXIII (1963).
13. *Forbes*, Vol. 98, No. 11 (December 1, 1966), p. 27.
14. Robert Grosse, "The Structure of Capital," in Wassily Leontief (ed.), *Studies in the Structure of the American Economy*, Oxford University Press, 1953.

machine tools. Much of the electronics industry is classified under electrical equipment.

A study of the United States economy in 1958 revealed eleven industries from an eighty-two–industry classification having at least 30 percent of their output directly assigned to gross private fixed capital formation: new construction; furniture and fixtures (other than household); farm machinery and equipment; construction, mining, and oil field machinery; materials handling machinery and equipment; metalworking machinery and equipment; special industry machinery and equipment; office, computing, and accounting machines; service industry machines; electric industrial equipment and apparatus; transportation equipment (other than motor vehicles and aircraft).[15]

No two studies use precisely the same industry classifications, but it is clear that capital goods flow from a small number of industrial groups, including the broad areas of new construction, metalworking machinery, electrical machinery, mass-transportation equipment, farm machinery, and office machines. Confining our attention to manufacturing, we shall ignore new construction.

3) INDUSTRIAL INTERDEPENDENCE—BACKWARD AND FORWARD LINKAGE: This might be called the Hirschman effect, for as Albert O. Hirschman shows, using the work of input-output specialists, industries with high backward and forward linkage furnish a peculiar growth-inducing pressure for other sectors.[16] In a study of economic interdependence in Italy, Japan, and the United States, Professors Chenery and Clark discovered that the following industries combined the highest levels of both backward linkage (the proportion of output representing purchases from other industries) and forward linkage (the proportion of output going to sectors other than final consumer demand): iron and steel, paper and products, petroleum products, nonferrous metals, chemicals, coal products, rubber products, textiles, and printing and publishing.[17] As Hirschman notes in his discussion of

15. Morris R. Goldman, Martin L. Marimont, Beatrice N. Vaccara, "The Interindustry Structure of the United States: A Report on the 1958 Input-Output Study," *Survey of Current Business*, Vol. 44 (November, 1964).
16. Albert O. Hirschman, *The Strategy of Economic Development*, Yale University Press, 1958, pp. 98–119.
17. Hollis B. Chenery and Paul G. Clark, *Interindustry Economics*, John Wiley & Sons, Inc., 1959, p. 207.

an early draft of the Chenery work, this ranking does injustice to machinery and transportation equipment.

4) PRICE-COST EFFECT ON OTHER INDUSTRIES: The price of a few materials exerts a large impact on the cost structure of other industries, thus affecting in turn their product prices and output levels. The most important price-cost effect is exercised by the steel industry. Steel price increases push up costs, for instance, in the machinery industry, affecting the supply price of capital assets and hence the aggregate rate of new investment. As Eckstein and Fromm wrote in an important study, "steel is an important input into many other industries. Thus, any price increase in steel ripples through the economy in the form of cost increases, leading to higher prices in other industries."[18] The aluminum industry exerts a similar though weaker effect, as, to some extent, does copper.

5) LEADING GROWTH SECTORS: The aggregate rate of national economic growth is the summation of individual industry rates of expansion and decline. The most rapidly expanding industries provide the momentum aiding the rise in gross national product. Ignoring the publicly regulated utilities, the most rapidly growing industries during the 1950's were electrical machinery, aircraft, instruments, chemicals, rubber, and plastics products.[19] During the expansive years 1961 through 1965, the following manufacturing industries (listed in order of magnitude) achieved increases in output well above the average: nonelectrical machinery, instruments, primary metals, fabricated metals, lumber and wood products, electrical machinery, furniture and fixtures, transportation equipment and ordinance, rubber and miscellaneous plastics, and chemicals and allied products.[20]

6) MAJOR RESEARCH AND DEVELOPMENT INDUSTRIES: A dominant factor in economic growth is technical innovation resulting from organized research and development. The bulk of American research and development effort outside agriculture is expended in the aircraft and missile, electrical equipment and communication, machinery, chemicals (particularly industrial

18. Otto Eckstein and Gary Fromm, *Steel and the Postwar Inflation*, Study Paper No. 2, Study of Employment, Growth and Price Levels, Joint Economic Committee (1959), p. 4.
19. Harold G. Vatter, *The U.S. Economy in the 1950's*, W. W. Norton & Company, Inc., 1963, p. 164.
20. U.S. Department of Commerce, "The Production Expansion in Perspective," *Survey of Current Business*, Vol. 46 (January, 1966), p. 14.

chemicals), and petroleum refining and extraction industries.[21]

7) WAGE-SETTING DEMONSTRATION EFFECT: Key wage bargains in a few industries tend to set the pace for wage rates elsewhere. Here again, steel is important: "Steel wages are determined in key wage bargains, often setting the pattern for other industries including, at times, automobiles, metalworking, fabricating, aluminum, and cement."[22] Eckstein and Wilson identified the following industries as "key groups" in postwar pattern bargaining: rubber; stone, clay, and glass; primary metals; fabricated metals; nonelectrical machinery; electrical machinery; transportation equipment; instruments; and industrial chemicals.[23] In a similar study, John Maher uncovered pace setting collective bargainers (Maher labeled these firms "central bargainers") in steel, automobiles, aluminum, farm machinery, electrical equipment, rubber, copper, aircraft, petroleum refining, meat packing, shipbuilding, and chemicals.[24]

8) FULL-EMPLOYMENT BOTTLENECK INDUSTRIES: The War Production Board's experience during the early months of World War II pinpointed potential bottlenecks to rapid economic expansion. Three major industrial raw materials—steel, copper, and aluminum—remained critical during the entire period, enabling the planning process to be based in part on this stability.[25] During peacetime, such bottlenecks tend to be reflected in rapidly rising prices for these products. Aluminum and copper price increases during the mid-1960's economic expansion prompted the release of supplies of these materials from government stockpiles. Rising prices in the steel industry have called forth government intervention and continuing government surveillance. During 1965, about two-fifths of the 1.3 percent rise in industrial commodity prices was the result of metals and metal products increases; nonferrous metals accounted for 70 percent of this rise.

21. National Science Foundation, *Industrial R and D Funds in Relation to Other Economic Variables,* Government Printing Office, 1964, p. 6.
22. Eckstein and Fromm, *op. cit.,* p. 4.
23. Otto Eckstein and Thomas A. Wilson, "The Determination of Money Wages in American Industry," *Quarterly Journal of Economics,* Vol. LXXVI, No. 3 (August, 1962), pp. 384–385, 394.
24. John E. Maher, "The Wage Pattern in the United States, 1946–1957," *Industrial and Labor Relations Review,* Vol. 15, No. 1 (October, 1961), p. 12.
25. D. Novick, M. L. Anshen, W. C. Truppner, *Wartime Production Controls,* Columbia University Press, 1949.

During December, 1965, six manufacturing industries were operating at or beyond preferred capacity utilization rates—nonferrous metals, fabricated metals and instruments, transportation equipment (other than trucks and autos), textiles, machinery, and rubber. Only nonferrous metals was operating above 100 percent capacity.[26]

Listing only those industries evincing at least two of our eight criteria, we discover the following "key" industries: machinery (including electrical), steel, nonferrous metals, transportation equipment (other than aircraft and automobiles), aircraft, chemicals (particularly industrial chemicals), rubber products, petroleum refining, electronics, automobiles, and instruments. Table 1 lists these industries in the manufacturing hub, giving the value of shipment concentration ratios for major four-digit subgroups in 1963.

TABLE 1.
*Key Industries, Percent of Value of Shipments
by Largest Producers, 1963*

	4 Largest	8 Largest
1. MACHINERY		
A. *Machine tools*		
1. metal-cutting machine tools	20	32
2. metal-forming machine tools	22	39
B. *Electrical machinery, excluding electronics*		
1. motors and generators	50	59
2. engine electrical equipment	69	79
3. electrical products, not elsewhere classified	38	48
C. *Farm machinery*		
1. farm machinery and equipment	43	55
D. *Miscellaneous machinery*		
1. construction machinery	42	53
2. internal combustion engines	49	65
3. computing and related machines	67	80
4. industrial trucks and tractors	54	61
2. IRON AND STEEL		
1. blast furnaces and steel mills	50	69
2. electrometallurgical products	79	95
3. steel pipe and tube	27	42
4. steel foundries	23	36

26. *Economic Report of the President,* January, 1966, Table 9, p. 68.

	4 Largest	8 Largest
3. NONFERROUS METALS		
A. *Aluminum*		
1. primary aluminum	n.a.	100
2. aluminum rolling and drawing	68	79
B. *Copper*		
1. primary copper	78	98
2. copper rolling and drawing	45	67
4. TRANSPORTATION EQUIPMENT, OTHER THAN AIRCRAFT AND AUTOMOBILES		
1. shipbuilding and repairing	48	63
2. locomotives and parts	97	99
3. railroad and street cars	53	73
5. AIRCRAFT		
1. aircraft	59	83
2. aircraft engines and parts	56	77
6. CHEMICALS, ESPECIALLY INDUSTRIAL		
1. alkalies and chlorine	62	88
2. industrial gases	72	86
3. intermediate coal tar products	54	70
4. inorganic pigments	68	84
5. organic chemicals, not elsewhere classified	51	63
6. inorganic chemicals, not elsewhere classified	31	49
7. cellulosic man-made fibers	82	100
7. RUBBER PRODUCTS		
1. tires and inner tubes	70	89
2. reclaimed rubber	93	100
8. PETROLEUM		
1. petroleum refining	34	56
2. lubricating oils and greases	36	48
9. ELECTRONICS		
1. radio, TV communication equipment	29	45
2. semiconductors	46	65
3. electronic components, not elsewhere classified	13	21
10. AUTOMOTIVE		
1. motor vehicles and parts	79	83
2. truck trailers	59	69
11. INSTRUMENTS		
1. scientific instruments	29	40
2. mechanical measuring devices	22	36
3. photographic equipment	63	76

SOURCE: U.S. Bureau of the Census, *Concentration Ratios in Manufacturing Industry, 1963,* Part I, Table 2, U.S. Government Printing Office, 1966.

Key Sectors: U.S. and Communist Versions

GIVEN the technical similarity of economic structures among industrial nations, we may find it instructive to check our list of key industries against those of the two leading Communist nations. Since it is physically impossible for central economic planners to allocate everything, Communist planners must confront head-on the problem of illuminating key sectors. The Soviets solve their allocation problems by maintaining strict powers of central allocation over a number of "funded" commodities, using these to exercise discretion over the rate and direction of productive effort throughout the economy. Funded commodities include the following: (1) most important producer goods, including ferrous and nonferrous metals, fuels, chemicals, etc.; (2) machinery and equipment; and (3) major materials used by consumer goods industries.[27] This list bears a striking resemblance to our own.

Professor Peter Wiles reproduces a Chinese classification of key sectors as follows:

1. Production of the means of production;
2. Production of motive power and fuels;
3. Production of raw materials required for producing "labor materials" [defined as the materials for (1), and the materials required to create "labor conditions": rails, metal structures, mine ventilating equipment, draining equipment, cement, etc., required for railways, factories, and warehouses];
4. Defense industry.[28]

Once again, the American manufacturing nucleus fits the Chinese classification rather well. The automobile industry, probably because abundant privately owned transportation is a luxury none but the richest industrial nations can afford, makes an uncomfortable alliance, although it harbors a fair share of U.S. defense production.

27. Herbert S. Levine, "The Centralized Planning of Supply in Soviet Industry," in Joint Economic Committee, *Comparisons of the United States and Soviet Economies*, Government Printing Office, 1959, p. 155.

28. Peter J. D. Wiles, *The Political Economy of Communism*, Basil Blackwell & Mott, Ltd., 1962, pp. 281–282.

Summary

OUR TWO-PART OUTLINE of the U.S. industrial system's technical anatomy is complete. First, we divided manufacturing techniques into three extensive categories: unit and small batch, large batch and mass, and process production. We noted that American output shifts towards an emphasis on continuous flow techniques—automated mass production and process production —as population and buying power expands. This trend has undoubtedly enhanced consumer welfare, all the more so if we assume that consumers have realized real satisfaction from mushrooming advertising outlays.

Next, we concentrated on the technical hierarchy of production. Finding that some sectors in the American economy are more important than others, we narrowed the search for critical industries to manufacturing. Within manufacturing, we developed eight criteria to illuminate significant industries, accepting as key industries only those sharing at least two of our standards. The eleven industries meeting this test were then compared to Russian and Chinese classifications of industrial importance; the correspondence was striking.

Unit and small batch production characterizes several of our key industries. Examples are found in machine tools, heavy electrical equipment, and transportation equipment (other than aircraft and automobile). Some key industries employ primarily large batch and mass production—the bulk of iron, steel and aluminum, copper, and automobiles—while still others, including continuous rolling iron, steel and aluminum mills, industrial chemicals, and petroleum are dependent on process techniques. In short, although mass and process production are found primarily in key industries, every production type is well-represented in the manufacturing core. How the technical structure's growth and performance are determined will be studied next as we turn our attention to the business organization of the U.S. economy.

4. The Business Organization of the U.S. Industrial System

If THE technical or production level of an economy can be likened to the bone structure of the human body, and key industries compared to the circulatory system, so business organizations can be viewed as the American economic nervous system. As the network of nerves controls the body, so the intricate web of business relations controls the private economy.

The human nervous system is divided into three parts: the central or cerebrospinal system, composed of the brain and spinal cord; the peripheral nervous system, comprising nerves and ganglia derived from the central nervous system; and the autonomic nervous system, including those nerves and ganglia which supply the walls of the vascular system and the various viscera and glands. It is tempting to equate the central nervous system with the center economy, the peripheral system with the periphery economy, and the autonomic system with social overhead capital. As the next three chapters will show, the analogy is a reasonably close one.

Unlike the Russian economy, where Gosplan, the central planning agency, directs the allocation of strategic resources, the U.S. economy has no visible seat of central control. A comparison between a human nervous system and the American economic system breaks down, then, if we equate the cerebrum or brain with the center economy, for an identifying mark of American economic life is the decentralization of economic decision. This dispersion of authority extending even into key industries is not without its advantages, as most Americans are aware. Creating rivalry and competition, at its best it is a spur to innovation and efficiency. Such dispersion of economic authority fosters a laissez faire of economic goals, enabling one firm to concentrate on sales with a profit restraint, another to stress research as internal funds allow, and perhaps a third to maximize profits in the short-run, neoclassical sense. Such goal permissiveness may be the despair of the economic theorist, but it evidently does the economy no substantial harm. What is most grievously damaged when planning errors occur is the firm (although lapses in wisdom are now unlikely to be fatal to the *center* firm); the industry will undoubtedly suffer little, and a competing center firm may even reap windfall gains from a brother company's misfortune. Montgomery Ward's caution in an expanding postwar economy set mass retailing back little, but it contributed to Sears's opulence.

But for all its virtues, the system is not without faults. The most glaring is economic instability. Were the center economy, rooted as it is in key industries, controlled by a single firm, business cycles and the resulting periodic unemployment would either disappear or take a hitherto unknown form. To compensate for a lack of managerial coordination in the economic center, the Federal government for the last thirty-five years has manipulated the money supply, Federal receipts, and Federal expenditures in an effort to *create* full employment, an environment of general economic welfare. But it has intervened in much the same way a clinical psychiatrist intervenes, *sotto voce*. Preferring not to take a dominating economic role, but only giving therapy to what must seem at times a multiple schizophrenia, the government watches over its economic subject. Providing a permissive environment in the creation of full employment, it has left the task of maintaining it to the center economy. But to maintain full employment without inflation, demand and capacity must be put into dynamic equilibrium, at least in key industries. And this cannot be accomplished through uncoordinated decision making in the central economic nervous system.

Lacking a central directory of economic decision, we say that "the market" guides production. And so it does. But "the market" is a difficult abstraction, and when explained by means of the accepted theory of supply and demand, it may leave a false impression about the center economy. It is clear that "the market" is a short-run concept. The market cannot plan. Consumers may, through their purchases, have a major decision in the allocation of resources, but they are ill-equipped to guide economic growth. Is there, then, no planning in a market economy, American-style? Quite the contrary. Much of the world's best economic planning takes place in America. What the United States economy lacks, so important to the French and Russian economies, is *coordinated* planning. In the United States center firms evolve intricate but highly flexible plans. But this firm level planning is never coordinated either on an industry basis, as in France, or on a national level, as in the Soviet Union. If industry level coordination does take place in the United States, it is in clear violation of the antitrust statutes. The strongest coordination in oligopolistic industries, being principally price and technical leadership by a dominant firm, might be called "consensus planning," but even this minor coordination is in a gray area legally and can only occur where the oligopolistic industry is relatively stable and well-disciplined.

Before we turn to the specifics of the American business system, let us call back the levels of economic order. We may best understand the distinction between the technical or production level of an economy and its organizational overlay by taking an imaginary flight over the world's industrial centers. Should you chance to journey by air over the industrial cities of North America, Western or Eastern Europe, the Soviet Union, or Japan, and should your flight proceed in this age of supersonic travel at a speed allowing you to observe the industrial sprawl below, you would view scenes of remarkable similarity. There would be differences, to be sure, natural and cultural, in the urban terrain, but were you momentarily granted X-ray vision, the technical skeleton and vital organs of developed economies would overshadow national peculiarities. The heart of the abundant industrial economy, in Tokyo or Toledo, is the factory system, pumping goods and the income to purchase them over the nation's roads and rails. The technical means of abundance are quite similar in all industrial countries. Industrial machinery works equally well, given adequate housing and care, in Leningrad or Louisville.

Granted an engineering similarity on the technical level, differences do exist and they are not without significance. To some degree machines and men are substitutes; hence men can replace expensive machinery where labor is cheap. Within well-defined limits, modern production can be labor- or capital-intensive. The decision to use more machines or additional men is commonly called the "substitution of factors at the margin." But such substitution can typically take place only at the margin, for men cannot totally replace machines nor can machines wholly replace men. The decision to use more of one or the other is a marginal decision made within usually narrow technical confines.

So it is that we may see, from our airborne seat, textiles being produced with considerable labor in Calcutta but almost totally by machine in North Carolina. If workers with the requisite skills are plentiful, and money for machinery scarce, production becomes labor-intensive. But machinery there must be, or there will be no modern industrial production. And without key industries to fill supply lines the nation becomes economically anemic.

On the technical level, where production takes place, industrial economies have much in common. Mature industrial economies probably vary less in their technical structure than do humans in bone structure. It is on the organizational level, where the control of production is exercised, that the most pronounced differences appear. The remainder of this chapter is devoted to an examination of the unique pattern of American business organization, including its division into the large-scale center economy and the smaller-scale periphery complex.

The Center Economy

ONE OF THE first things we notice about the diverse manufacturing industries listed in Table 1 is their characteristically high degree of concentration. Taking an average, we find that among the 42 subgroups the four largest firms produced 52 percent of the value of shipments in 1963. The largest eight firms accounted for an average of 67 percent. Using the Kaysen-Turner criteria for determining market concentration, we find that only two of our forty-two industries fall within the unconcentrated, non-oligopolistic range. Twenty-nine of the 42 industries are type I oligopolies, described by Kaysen and Turner as markets where "recognition of interdependence by leading firms is extremely likely, and the 75 percent share of the first twenty sellers makes it likely that the response of the smaller sellers will not limit the behavior of the larger firms." [1]

Center firms found in key U.S. manufacturing industries have much in common. Manufacturing is their major concern; they characteristically operate in highly concentrated markets; they are large in terms of assets, income, expenditures, sales, and employment; they service national and even international markets; they have achieved at least partial vertical integration; and they tend toward product diversification. But there are important differences, and these may prove more instructive for our purposes than similarities. No two companies are exactly alike in corporate style or organization, yet the relentless pressure of common market forces imposes recognizable patterns on most firms sharing similar market-orientations. While guarding against casuistic classification, we can meaningfully divide key industries into four broad market-orientation types: intermediate goods manufacture, raw material processing, government sales, and consumer sales. Perhaps if we include the number of firms dominating each industry within the four market-orientation types, we can gain insight into the complex relationship between the large-firm center economy and the key industries within the U.S. economy.

1. Intermediate Goods Manufacture • The manufacturers of intermediate goods include the machinery groups—machine tools, heavy electrical, and farm—as well as transportation equipment, industrial chemicals, and instruments. Machine tools provide an

---

1. Carl Kaysen and Donald F. Turner, *Antitrust Policy: An Economic and Legal Analysis,* Harvard University Press, 1959, p. 27.

interesting exception to the key industries' concentration rule. The industry is highly competitive and almost all firms are small. Perhaps machine tools can best be viewed as an anachronism, a remnant of a vanished era when even key industries were composed of small firms. Or perhaps the distinction of technological convergence having passed to more vital areas, machine tools should no longer be included among those occupying the economic heartland. In any event, three major merger movements have left machine tools free of center firm control.

The electrical industry makes a striking contrast. Two giant firms, General Electric and Westinghouse, dominate most electrical fields, followed by the smaller Radio Corporation of America and Sylvania Electric (a branch of General Telephone). All four are decentralized and highly diversified. American farm machinery production is lorded by the big three—International Harvester, Allis-Chalmers, and Deere and Company, followed by J. I. Case, Ford Motor, and White Motor.

Transportation equipment (excluding private transportation) is concentrated by product. The leaders include such firms as ACF Industries, Alco Products, Baldwin-Lima-Hamilton, and General American Transportation Company. Most are diversified; ACF Industries, for instance, combines the production of railway cars with electronics.

In chemicals, a relatively small number of large, diversified companies share the bulk of U.S. output in the various product classifications. The chemical industry retains a classic intermediate goods orientation; since the major raw materials of chemical manufacture are themselves chemicals, the industry becomes its own most important market. Leading firms include DuPont, the world's largest chemical company; Union Carbide; Dow Chemical; Olin Mathieson Chemical; Allied Chemical; Monsanto Chemical; and American Cyanamid. Leading nonchemical firms in the chemical business include W. R. Grace, Standard Oil (N.J.), Phillips Petroleum, Eastman Kodak, Goodrich Rubber, and Pittsburgh Plate and Glass.

The instruments industry covers a wide variety of firms, characterized on the one hand by Eastman Kodak and Minnesota Mining and Manufacturing, and on the other by the Harris

Timer Company of Milwaukee, a firm of perhaps fifty employees producing spring and electrically driven timing devices. Several products in the instrument category are produced by a handful of the largest American firms, while others are manufactured by moderate size enterprises.

2. *Raw Material Processing* • The raw material processing group is composed of steel, aluminum, and copper. The steel industry is led by U.S. Steel, followed by eleven other integrated companies comprising the remainder of steel's big twelve. These dozen industry leaders control over 80 percent of U.S. productive capacity in pig iron, steel ingots, and finished hot-rolled steel. Aluminum is dominated by the three giants—Alcoa, Reynolds, and Kaiser. Together they account for over 90 percent of alumina capacity, 88 percent of ingot capacity, and from 40 to 90 percent of U.S. output potential in the various types of aluminum mill shapes. The big four in copper—Kennecott Copper, Anaconda, Phelps Dodge, and American Smelting and Refining—produce about 90 percent of the nation's copper. In short, the three raw material industries are dominated by nineteen firms, with twelve of them in steel.

The raw material industries are model intermediate goods producers. The automobile industry alone accounts for about 20 percent of domestic steel consumption. Firms within each industry produce largely homogeneous products. Until quite recently, raw material firms were managerially passive, retaining a centralized bureaucracy and diversifying little outside their basic product lines. Steel firms in particular have behaved more like a family than aggressive business enterprises. [THOMAS F. PATTON, President, Republic Steel — *For many years there existed a deeply entrenched attitude among steelmakers that there was very little they could do to increase the nation's total steel requirements. We were limited, so it was believed, by a "derived demand"—in other words, a demand derived from the activity of our customers. It was thus left largely up to them to whet the public appetite for their products made of steel.*] [2]

In recent years, the growth of raw material substitution be-

2. *Forbes,* Vol. 93, No. 5 (March 1, 1964), p. 24.

tween aluminum, steel, copper, and new varieties of plastics
have eroded traditional markets, making raw material firms
more price and advertising conscious. Penetration pricing is now
widely practiced outside steel, setting prices so that one's own
product can pierce another raw material's marginal markets.

3. *Government Sales* • Firms in the government sales group
use the Federal government as their primary market, furnishing
the implements of national defense. They serve an essentially
one-customer market, although different segments of the Department of Defense procure different items. Price plays a decidedly secondary role; scientific achievement, founded on
large-scale research and development, is of primary consequence.

Aircraft and electronics are oriented toward government
sales. The aircraft industry is compressed into a few firms, including United Aircraft, General Dynamics, Lockheed Aircraft,
North American Aviation, Boeing, Douglas Aircraft, Grumman
Aircraft Engineering, and Republic Aircraft. Attempts at diversification by aircraft companies have generally proved un-
successful; for example, in 1961, North American Aviation did
97 percent of its business with the government, General Dynamics about 70 percent.

The electronics market is better diversified. In addition to military sales, electronic firms serve industrial buyers, households,
and a replacement parts market. But the increase in military demand accounted for about two-thirds of sales growth during the
1950's. Without the impetus of government demand, electronics
would not have been a leading growth industry. The seven
firms with over one-half billion dollars' worth of electronics
revenue yearly are Radio Corporation of America, General
Electric, Western Electric, Sperry Rand, Hughes Aircraft, IBM,
and Raytheon.[3]

4. *Consumer Sales* • Key industries characterized by the production of consumer goods include the private transportation
group—automobiles, rubber, and petroleum. Firms in these industries, like those in most other key industries, defy easy

---

3. Charles E. Silberman, "The Coming Shakeout in Electronics," *Fortune* (August, 1960), p. 189.

classification. The basic automotive product, private passenger cars, is clearly not an intermediate good, although subsidiary sales of trucks and busses can be so considered, as can company-owned cars. The industry is not primarily a processor of raw materials, yet backward integration has brought some processing activity under the control of automotive corporations. Automotive firms are not heavily dependent on government contracts, even though General Motors, Ford, and Chrysler were among the top thirty-one prime defense contractors in 1963.[4]

It is their extensive diversification, decentralization, geographic dispersion, vertical integration, and international scope which makes the major U.S. auto firms perfect center firms. As is common in key industries, the automobile industry is dominated by a big three—General Motors, Ford, and Chrysler. Indeed, it is for all practical purposes composed of only the big three and the little one, American Motors.

Petroleum and rubber companies usually sell to final consumers through the medium of company-owned or franchised outlets. Following a common center-firm pattern, petroleum and rubber enterprises are diversifying their operations into other industries, most noticeably the related chemical industry.

Petroleum is dominated by the twenty majors, including such well-known firms as Texaco, Standard Oil (N.J.), Gulf Oil Corporation, Shell Oil Company, Standard Oil (Calif.), Socony Mobil Oil, Standard Oil (Indiana), Phillips Petroleum, Citgo (formerly Cities Service), and Sinclair Oil. Rubber is the province of a big four—Uniroyal (formerly U.S. Rubber), B. F. Goodrich, Goodyear Tire and Rubber, and Firestone Tire and Rubber. The use of private brands on the products of major producers in the last several years has created considerable confusion in the tire market, obscuring the former importance of trade names.

Center Firms and Key Industries: Summary

OUR FINDINGS can be briefly summarized. Within the population of American business firms, a relatively small number of economic giants form an economy apart, creating and reacting to

---

4. Joint Economic Committee, *Background Materials on Economic Aspects of Military Procurement and Supply—1964,* Government Printing Office, 1964, p. 13.

economic forces differing in substance from those impinging on
their smaller rivals. We have named this economy of elite firms
"the center economy." In addition, we have noted that the economic structure of a developed country exhibits a hierarchy of
industrial importance. Following convention, we have called
those industries occupying the commanding heights of the economy "key industries." The key industries reveal extraordinary
levels of concentration; almost all are oligopolistic, many are
dominated by three or four firms. Thus the "displacement effect"
of removing the two leading enterprises from the electrical industry, the top three from farm machinery, the dominant trio
from aluminum, the commanding four from copper, the largest
quartet from rubber, and the big three from automobiles would
be almost total. *Should these nineteen business organizations suddenly disappear, six of our key industries would virtually vanish.*
Table 2 confirms the close association among center firms when
conservatively defined as the 200 largest industrial corporations
and key industries. In only three of the twenty industries listed
does the percentage of center firm employment fall below one-
third.

TABLE 2.

*Share of Employment Accounted for by 200 Largest
Manufacturing Companies in Key Industries, 1958*

	Percent Employment by 200 Largest Firms
A. PRIMARY METAL PRODUCTS	
1. steel mills	80.4
2. nonferrous metals	44.4
3. primary metals, not elsewhere classified	32.3
B. TRANSPORTATION EQUIPMENT	
1. aircraft	94.6
2. motor vehicles and equipment	70.6
3. aircraft parts	66.5
4. ships and boats	39.3
5. other transportation equipment	38.2
C. MACHINERY (except electrical)	
1. office and store machines	55.8
2. engines and turbines	53.1
3. service and household machines	41.9

	Percent Employment by 200 Largest Firms
4. tractors, farm and construction machinery	37.8
5. general industrial machinery	21.6
D. ELECTRICAL MACHINERY	
1. communication equipment	47.9
2. other electrical machinery	35.4
3. electrical industrial apparatus	34.8
E. CHEMICALS (*inorganic and organic*)	72.6
F. PETROLEUM (*petroleum refining*)	67.2
G. RUBBER PRODUCTS	49.5
H. INSTRUMENTS (*optical, etc.*)	30.7

SOURCE: U.S. Senate, Committee on the Judiciary, *Economic Concentration, Part I, Overall and Conglomerate Aspects,* Table E, 1964, p. 218.

The largest 200 U.S. corporations accounted for 60 percent or more of total employment in six industries: steel, inorganic and organic chemicals, motor vehicles, aircraft, petroleum refining, and aircraft parts. They employed between 40 and 59 percent of all workers in ten additional industries: rubber products; tobacco manufacturers; pulp, paper, and board; communication equipment; glass products; office and store machines; engines and turbines; service and household machines; nonferrous smelting and refining; drugs and medicines.[5] All of the first six industries, and half of the next ten, clearly qualify as key industries.

The influence of particular center firms in specific key industries is large, but the center-firm–key-industry link is stronger still. While continuing to show a dominant presence in their mother industries, center firms have spread beyond home industry bounds through diversification and integration. Several center firms loom large in more than one key industry. Where research and development are important—as in electrical machinery, chemicals, rubber, petroleum, and electronics—diversification is omnipresent. But industrial encroachment is not confined to high R and D firms. One of the farm machinery big three is a major electrical machinery producer; another has long been a leading

5. U.S. Senate, Committee on the Judiciary, *Economic Concentration, Part I, Overall and Conglomerate Aspects,* 1964, pp. 213–219.

truck and industrial machinery manufacturer. Rubber and petroleum firms are moving into chemicals.

The New Breed: Conglomerates

DURING THE past fifteen years a new breed of firm has forced its way into the center economy. Unlike most center firms, the core of these new enterprises is not a product line, nor even a single industry. The most recent initiates into the center economy are *pure conglomerates*. They fit into none of our product categories because they are not built around a specific market. Some of the more spectacular include Textron, Litton Industries, F.M.C., and Martin-Marietta. Minnesota Mining and Manufacturing also exhibits many pure conglomerate characteristics, even though it retains several of its traditional products.

Through merger these new titans have matured early. Litton has bought some fifty different companies during the past dozen years, enabling it to sell more than 500 items produced in 145 plants located in twenty-one states and twelve foreign countries. Originally specializing in electronics, Litton has diversified through such major acquisitions as Monroe Calculator ($25 million in assets), Cole Steel Equipment Company ($13 million), Royal-McBee, and the American Book Company. Other product acquisitions are spread from pressure-sensitive adhesive tape (Simon Adhesive Products, assets $1 million) to nuclear-powered submarines and offshore drillings rigs (Ingalls Shipbuilding, assets $16 million).

Textron, the sixty-first (1966) largest U.S. industrial enterprise, began in textiles but now holds no textile interests. Instead, Textron manufactures in five major product categories: agrochemicals, 11 percent of sales; consumer, 16 percent; aerospace, 36 percent; industrial, 20 percent; metal products, 17 percent (percentages are for 1965). Textron's thirty operating divisions make an enormous diversity of products, including machine tools, watchbands, industrial fasteners, chicken feed, helicopters, bathroom fixtures, chain saws, roller bearings, electronic equipment, and paint. Large acquisitions include Spencer Kellogg (assets $52 million), Bell Aircraft (assets $32 million), and

Benada Aluminum ($20 million). By buying Caroline Farms in 1963, Textron moved into the poultry business to insure a captive market for Beacon, Textron's feed-producing division. Carried to its logical extreme, the pure conglomerate could become an economy unto itself. [RUPERT C. THOMPSON, Chairman, Textron *— Except for the problem of acquiring management, there is no limit to how far we can go with this type of organization.*][6]

F.M.C. manufactures food industry machinery, insecticides, water treatment equipment, high-speed centrifugal pumps, oil field machinery, and a variety of other products. With the absorption of American Viscose (assets $335 million), giant F.M.C. literally swallowed a fellow giant.

With strong and permanent attachments to no principal industry or product, the pure conglomerate is the ultimate center firm. It may be formed around a research staff, like Minnesota Mining and Manufacturing, or innovative management like Textron. [RUPERT C. THOMPSON, Chairman, Textron *— Basically, Textron shouldn't be regarded as a manufacturing operation at all, but as a management concept like Litton or FMC. That's the secret of our success and that's where our basic strength lies.*][7] Following the successful center pattern pioneered by General Motors and DuPont, Textron's primary managerial weapon is its rigid control of divisional finances. Every year each Textron division prepares a twelve-month budget and a five-year forecast. The budget is checked monthly by top Textron management against operating results, then revised on a quarterly basis. Each division has its own staff for accounting, advertising, engineering, marketing and research, but the Textron general staff sets corporate guidelines and provides capital for new projects, as well as general accounting, legal, and planning services.

Like other successful diversified firms, pure conglomerates are highly decentralized, leaving initiative at levels well below top management. [ROY L. ASH, President, Litton Industries *— We are decentralized, period. We grew up decentralized. We leave acquired companies alone because it is ridiculous to make every-*

6. *Forbes*, Vol. 96, No. 11 (December 1, 1965), p. 36.
7. *Ibid.*, p. 32.

thing conform to one pattern. You destroy everything that was there.] [8] As the Federal government manages the national economy with the subtle techniques of monetary and fiscal policy, so the managers of these private economies within the economy wield only general financial powers. [ROY L. ASH, President, Litton Industries — *We elect to manage by not managing. We have one rule—there is no rule. And our policy is we have no firm policy. What is there left for management to do? The management of capital.*] [9]

At present pure conglomerates are impressive in size but few in number. But this new form of flexible center organization seems ideally suited to the technically dynamic, ever changing U.S. economy. [ROY L. ASH, President, Litton — *There are limitless opportunities for us to do new things which develop new markets and create new business.*] [10] Unless existing center firms speed their diversification pace, the economy's demand for pure conglomerates seems likely to continue exceeding the supply for a few more years. [TEX THORNTON, Chairman, Litton Industries — *We don't have enough big, broad-based companies in America to introduce to the market the fruits of our new technology, and to take the risk that this involves. Why, we have only about 20 industrial companies in the whole country with more that $2 billion in sales.*] [11] But profitable gaps in business organization are soon filled. A new crop of pure conglomerates is already rising to emulate the success of their predecessors. For example, the Standard International Corporation of Andover, Mass., is following the conglomerate pattern of assembling disparate firms and wielding strong financial control while giving managerial advice. SIC products already range from household cleaners and medical instruments to pumps and religious supplies. And SIC is now competing with older conglomerates for new acquisitions. [DANIEL E. HOGAN, JR., President, SIC — *We look for businesses that lend themselves to good orthodox management practices.*] [12]

Virtually all center firms have achieved considerable back-

8. *Business Week*, No. 1911 (April 16, 1966), p. 180.
9. *Ibid.*
10. *Forbes*, Vol. 93, No. 7 (April 1, 1964), p. 15.
11. *Forbes*, Vol. 96, No. 11 (December 1, 1965), p. 16.
12. *Forbes*, Vol. 97, No. 12 (June 15, 1966), p. 23.

ward and/or forward integration.[13] The raw material processing firms—those in steel, aluminum, and copper—own substantial portions of their raw material deposits. Petroleum and rubber, selling directly to final consumers, are integrated forward as well—the petroleum firms, with significant exceptions, stop with wholesaling, the rubber concerns extend into retailing. The major chemical firms have fully integrated production complexes, while the automotive companies supply many of their own input needs.

Center Firms and the International Economy

WHILE playing their critical role in the American economy, several center firms have broadened considerably their international base. Most center firms operate in more than one country, but a few receive at least half of their income or earnings from foreign sales—for example, Standard Oil of New Jersey (fifty-seven foreign affiliates), Socony Mobil, National Cash Register, Singer, and Burroughs. Several others make from 30 to 50 percent of their sales abroad, including Eastman Kodak, Caterpillar Tractor, International Harvester, and Minnesota Mining and Manufacturing. These are companies without a country, making managerial decisions based on world-wide alternatives. Table 3 lists a number of center firms located in key American industries but enjoying foreign sales of $100 million or more *or* selling at least a quarter of their output abroad.

In a few cases the same center firms are a major force in key European and American production. Automobiles exert such force. Ford makes 40 percent of its cars outside the U.S., Chrysler almost a third, General Motors about 20 percent. GM and Ford produce nearly two of every five cars in Germany. American and British firms dominate German oil refining; one-third of Germany's farm machinery is manufactured by three American companies and one British company. The truly multinational center firm, freed of exclusive dependence on a single national economy, is yet another manifestation of center managerial flexibility and planning. As the new, industry-flexible pure conglom-

13. Michael Gort, *Diversification and Integration in American Industry*, Princeton University Press, 1962, p. 79.

TABLE 3

*Center Firms with Foreign Sales Exceeding $100 Million
or Accounting for at Least 25 Percent of Total Sales, 1964*

AUTOMOTIVE—RUBBER
Chrysler
Firestone Tire
Ford Motor
General Motors
Goodyear Tire

MACHINERY
Caterpillar Tractor
Deere and Company
International Harvester
United Shoe Machinery

CHEMICALS
American Cyanamid
Celanese
Dow Chemical
E. I. DuPont
Eastman Kodak
Minnesota Mining and
   Manufacturing
Monsanto
Union Carbide

ELECTRICAL
General Electric
Sperry Rand

NONFERROUS METALS
American Smelting
Anaconda
Kennecott Copper

OFFICE EQUIPMENT—ELECTRONICS
IBM
Litton Industries
National Cash Register

PETROLEUM
Gulf
Socony Mobil
Standard Oil (N.J.)
Standard Oil (California)
Texaco

SOURCE: *Forbes,* Vol. 96, No. 1 (July 1, 1965), pp. 30–31.

erates join their center economy colleagues in abandoning a single national base, a potent hybrid business organization is born, floating free of traditional restraints, dependent solely on finesse and finance, management and money.

A major commodity in trade between industrial nations is the ability to embrace and merchandise new technology. And it is precisely here that the more progressive American center firms enjoy an international advantage. The American organizational center's invasion of Europe is now creating major problems for U.S. labor unions and antitrust policy.

We must keep a clear distinction between center firms and key industries. Not all firms in key industries are dominant firms, and many suppliers of factor inputs to dominant center firms are separate legal entities. Center firms dominate, but are not synonymous with, most key industries. For a complete description of the manufacturing-distributing economy, we must consider the role played by the periphery economy and its members.

The Periphery Economy

PERIPHERY FIRMS can be grouped under three broad headings according to their relationship with the economic center—satellites, loyal opposition, and free agents.

1. *Satellites* • Satellitic firms can be divided into two general groups, backward satellites and forward satellites. Backward satellites operate on the factor market side of center firms, supplying them with material inputs. Forward satellites function on the product market side, channeling the center firms' output toward its final buyer. In the automobile industry, for example, upholstery firms selling to auto manufacturers are backward satellites, automobile dealers are forward satellites. Backward satellites usually enjoy a locational advantage from proximity to the center firm. Their principal output is a minor input to the center firm, and their minimum economic size is much smaller than that of the center firm's industry. Prime government contracts typically go to center firms who subcontract them to backward satellites.

In the government-sales oriented aerospace industry, the relationships between center firm and satellite are highly structured and formal. The center firm plays the role of prime contractor, bearing the responsibility for developing and delivering the finished product. Prime contracting aerospace firms now fall into two groups: (1) the eleven remaining airframe manufacturers, and (2) a small group of electronics firms holding prime contracts for the smaller guided missiles. In many cases a brother center firm becomes an associate prime contractor, manufacturing propulsion units for rockets and power plants for aircraft.

Satellites are composed of subcontractors who manufacture systems and subsystems. Prime contractors obtain higher average profit rates than do subcontractors. The prime contractor receives in addition a management fee, based on a percentage of the value of the subcontract it awards, for supervising the work of subcontractors and integrating the subsystems. As prime contractors, center firms exercise the useful make-or-buy option —they can retain any part of the contract within the center firm that promises to be highly profitable.[14]

Economic satellites are operationally integrated into the activities of center firms, but they fall outside the corporate hierarchy. Advantages accruing to center firms from this arrangement compared to satellite ownership include: (1) transference of some business risk; (2) flexibility of operations; (3) low-cost maintenance of excess industry capacity during slack periods; (4) capital savings—funds can be invested in more useful or profitable pursuits; (5) advantages under antitrust laws; (6) avoidance of problems of fringe benefits for periphery owner and his employees, and circumvention of a multitude of union problems; (7) good public relations, as suggested in the phrase, "big business helps support small business." Forward satellites can often maintain good local contacts and favorable community relations somewhat difficult for a large "foreign" corporation to establish.

Many manufacturing satellites are "floating" satellites, dependent on sales to a key industry or set of key industries but not to a single center firm. "Attached" satellites are tied by contract, tradition, personal contacts, or some other means to a single or, more commonly, a small group of center firms. The demand for satellitic firm output is derived from the demand for the center firm's product, but the satellitic firm is totally isolated from the center firm's market. Satellitic firms sometimes receive financial assistance from their center patron, creating tangible avenues of influence and control. But in any event, major decision-making power stays with the center; control may be tentative and weak, but when exerted it emanates from the center.

In rare cases, center firms use divisions of other center firms as

14. Herman O. Stekler, *The Structure and Performance of the Aerospace Industry*, University of California Press, 1965, pp. 115–117.

satellites, creating a situation of countervailing power. A branch plant in one of the aluminum big three supplying a branch plant of one of the automotive big three provides one example. When center firm satelliting occurs, many advantages of flexibility and financial leverage are lost to the master firm.

2. *The Loyal Opposition* · Sometimes called the competitive fringe, the loyal opposition is made up of nondominant firms providing competition for center firms within their home industry. Loyal opposition firms customarily have most, though rarely all, of the following characteristics:

1) Heavy reliance on local sources of factor supply;

2) Technically inferior equipment;

3) Less integration than dominant firms;

4) In an industry enjoying foreign business, loyal opposition does not participate in such business, or receives a disproportionately small share;

5) Where sales promotion is an important factor, the loyal opposition is often confined to restricted markets—national and regional markets are more responsive to mass advertising;

6) The loyal opposition is typically a one-plant firm or a single or few-product firm;

7) The loyal opposition has a shorter life span than center firms, often ending life through center firm acquisition;

8) The loyal opposition typically surrenders power to make price decisions to center firms;

9) However, the loyal opposition is sometimes disloyal—when price stabilization is disrupted, loyal opposition firms are usually the disrupters;

10) Where nonprice competition predominates, the loyal opposition is the primary representative of price competition;

11) Taken as a group, the loyal opposition shows lower profit levels than center firms.[15]

3. *Free Agents* · "Free agents" is a residual category encompassing firms "free" of center affiliation, formal or informal. Most free

15. For a good discussion of these characteristics as they relate to the butter, flour, automobile, and glass container industries, see Harold G. Vatter, *Small Enterprise and Oligopoly*, Oregon State College Press, 1955, pp. 109–111.

agents operate on the economic fringes of the raw material processing—finished manufacture—retailing continuum, filling in production cracks and crannies. Such firms cannot integrate easily in either direction; the limited size of their market severely restricts scale economies for the plant, though they may exist for the firm. Manufacturing free agents often specialize in producing unique articles or unique batches of articles. Most firms relying primarily on discontinuous production, for instance, a job printer, qualify as free agents. Small-scale retailers may, through cooperatives, receive many scale economies through volume buying and mass advertising, allowing them to compete satisfactorily with retailing satellites while maintaining "free agent" status. Most free agents are necessarily small, suffering the numerous disadvantages attendant upon the small, local firm in an increasingly mobile national market.

Center Retailing

INDUSTRIAL placement has been an important factor in the evolution of U.S. corporate giants. It can hardly be that accident originally located most of the center firms in key manufacturing industries, particularly when scale economies are so significant in these areas. But it is economic size, not industrial location, that defines firms in the center economy. To complete our list of center firm types, we must add an additional category of large enterprises oriented toward neither intermediate goods manufacture, nor raw material processing, nor government sales. Our final group of center economy participants originated in *retailing* and continue to exhibit a retailing orientation. They entered manufacturing by way of vertical integration. In both general merchandising and grocery retailing, a core of large firms casts lengthy economic shadows, using small manufacturing enterprises as backward satellites.

Sears, Roebuck provides an excellent example of a retailing-oriented center firm. Like other retailers, Sears buys some of its merchandise from large, well-known manufacturers who remain primarily dependent on periphery outlets. Professor Galbraith uses one such case to illustrate countervailing power in retailing.[16] But unlike periphery retailers, Sears purchases about one-third of its merchandise, including most of its major appliance lines, under long-term buying arrangements with firms relying on Sears for a large share of total sales. These are normally small manufacturers. In addition, Sears holds stock interest in a number of firms (forty-six companies with 109 factories in 1954) selling large portions of their output to Sears.

Sears's movement into manufacturing is illustrated by their paint and wallpaper procurement. In 1956 Sears consolidated all its paint and wallpaper operations in a small, struggling company named Union Wallpaper. Sears installed a member of their own management, Sam U. Greenberg, then general manager of Sears's paint division, as president of the newly acquired firm. The name of Union Wallpaper was changed to Desoto Chemical Coatings in 1959. [GREENBERG — *Sears has found that an independent company functions more aggressively and efficiently than a division.*] [17] Sears represented 60 percent of Desoto sales in 1965, owning just over half of Desoto's common stock and all its preferred.

Sears owns a substantial interest in a number of other major suppliers, including Whirlpool (8.5 percent), whose sales to Sears (two-thirds of Whirlpool's output) give them the largest single share of the home-laundry equipment market, George Roper Corp. (59 percent), Armstrong Rubber (8.8 percent), Globe-Union (12 percent), and the Kellwood Company (18.3 percent). [RICHARD S. BURKE, former assistant to Sears's President, now Chairman, George Roper Corp. — *We've shown that we have the knowhow and the efficiency to manufacture to Sears' rigid specifications and still make a very satisfactory profit. Selling to Sears is a good business for companies that know how to do it.*] [18] Whether facing manufacturers as part owner or merely large buyer, Sears's marketing potential as exemplified by over 753 retail outlets, 970 catalogue offices, fifty-four telephone offices, eleven catalogue order plants, and eleven major warehouses allows the 350 or so Sears buyers to determine the design

16. John Kenneth Galbraith, *American Capitalism,* Sentry Edition, Houghton Mifflin Company, 1962, p. 119.

17. *Forbes,* Vol. 95, No. 8 (April 15, 1965), p. 31.

18. *Forbes,* Vol. 98, No. 2 (July 15, 1966), p. 29.

and product specifications for the $5 billion worth of Sears merchandise sold yearly. [AUSTIN T. CUSHMAN, Sears Chairman — *The modern Sears must be seen primarily as a system for the distribution of goods and services, the channels being catalogue order and retail sales.*] [19] Other general merchandising center firms include J. C. Penney, Montgomery Ward, F. W. Woolworth, Federated Department Stores, W. T. Grant, and J. J. Newberry.

As Sears is to general merchandising, so A & P's fame is to grocery retailing (4,585 stores in 1965). But while Sears has steadily expanded, A & P has fallen into relative decline. A & P's share of grocery chain sales fell from 35.8 percent in 1940 to 26.6 percent in 1958. Yet A & P still retains a position of prominence in the industry. A & P operated in 152 of the 177 metropolitan areas in the U.S. during 1963. By comparison Safeway Stores, the second largest grocery chain, operated in only sixty-three metropolitan areas. In thirty-nine of these cities (26 percent) A & P was first in grocery sales, and in all but thirty-one (21 percent) A & P ranked among the top four grocery retailers. There were 790 grocery chains with four or more stores in 1958, the fifty largest accounting for 90 percent of chain sales. Grocery retailing is divided into three organizational types: corporate chains with 43 percent of 1958 sales, voluntary and cooperative chains with 41.6 percent of sales, and unaffiliated independents mustering only 15.4 percent of the 1958 total.

On a national basis, the twenty largest corporate chains together with the twenty largest voluntary and cooperative chain members sell over half the nation's groceries. Since 55 percent of the voluntary and cooperative chains operate in only one state and only 5.8 percent serve over four states, regional concentration is much greater than the national figures suggest. Willard F. Mueller and Leon Garoian's thorough study of grocery markets indicates that within regions and inside cities with population over 25,000, the four largest corporate chains together with the four largest noncorporate chains account for two-thirds of all grocery sales.[20] Within individual retailing areas, grocery sales are

---

19. *Forbes,* Vol. 97, No. 1 (January 1, 1966), p. 111.
20. The statistics on grocery retailing are taken from Willard F. Mueller and Leon

firmly held by the big eight. The largest grocery chains do not always limit their operations to food retailing. During 1963 twelve of the top twenty grocery chains owned nonfood stores, primarily discount houses and drug stores. And six of the leading twenty chains sponsored affiliated independent retail grocers; twelve made sales to other food retailers and to food wholesalers.

Large-scale grocery retailing, like other forms of large retailing, leads into manufacturing. In 1958, sixty-two grocery chains operated 326 food manufacturing plants producing products worth $1.3 billion at wholesale; 85 percent of the output of these plants was sold through the parent chain stores. Over 90 percent of these chain-owned plants were operated by the twenty largest corporate chains; the four largest operate more manufacturing plants than all other chains combined. By 1963, the forty largest food chains manufactured food products valued at $1.8 billion; half of this total ($897 billion) was produced in plants owned by the four largest chains. Between 1954 and 1963 the value of food products manufactured by the forty leading chains increased by 51 percent. Product specification decisions are, of course, the responsibility of the retailers in these establishments.

Galbraith's theory of countervailing power recognizes the economic potential of large-scale retailing, but his analysis stresses only one aspect of center retailing procurement—purchases by center retailers from center suppliers. Increasingly, center retailers are shifting to periphery manufacturing firms for merchandise, commonly placing these small suppliers in a satellitic state through ownership or long-term contract. The retailing center does not characteristically countervail the power of the manufacturing center; it establishes instead a largely self-sufficient syndrome buttressed by a community of manufacturing satellites. The National Commission on Food Marketing report provides a concise summary of the economic resiliency characteristic to center firms:

> In the short run small companies often appear to be bettering their large conglomerate rivals. For a time the

Garoian, *Changes in the Market Structure of Grocery Retailing,* University of Wisconsin Press, 1961, and from National Commission on Food Marketing, *Organization and Competition in Food Retailing,* Technical Study No. 7, U.S. Government Printing Office, 1966.

supermarket revolution, spawned by small companies in the early 1930's, threatened to undermine the position of large chains; but today the 20 largest chains, alone, operate well over one-half of all supermarkets. The growth of large chains appeared stunted by World War II; but by 1948 they had recaptured their prewar position. Most recently, the position of the large chains appeared threatened by the food discount department, which was pioneered by smaller companies in the late 1950's; but in the last 4 years the largest chains have captured a sizeable portion of this business.

❋   ❋   ❋

Large chains, as a group, have withstood successfully each of these and other innovations. Over the past two decades, not only have large chains expanded their sales in absolute terms, but the 20 largest have expanded, almost continuously, their share of sales since World War II; it is not clear, however, that they would have done so had they not made numerous mergers during the period.[21]

Center Economic Advantages

THE INCLUSION of retailing center firms reinforces our insistence that center influence on periphery conduct springs ultimately from differences in economic size. Large firms in the center economy, both in manufacturing and in retailing, are endowed with the following advantages:

1) Center firms have extensive assets, allowing them to outspend and outlose periphery firms;

2) Vertical integration allows center firms to underbid free agent and forward satellite retailers for large contracts—center firm profits can be realized at the manufacturing level;

3) Center firms must deal carefully with other center firms—a war between them would hurt both; center firms may also consider the welfare of periphery firms, but when an economic

21. National Commission on Food Marketing, *op. cit.*, p. 415.

crisis develops, small rivals and suppliers are expendable—a situation not unlike that between wealthy and poor nations;

4) Center firms maintain better geographic and product diversification—thus center firms can withstand losses in one area or on one product indefinitely;

5) The center firm can become its own supplier and distributor—the question of satellite ownership is one of administrative choice;

6) Center firms can spread risks and carry their own insurance, and sometimes provide portions of their own transportation needs;

7) When demand is slack, consumers are likely to prefer familiar brands, forcing loyal opposition firms to suffer a disproportionate share of the total sales reductions; hence the loyal opposition provides a buffer against the full impact of a market downturn;

8) Center buyers often receive the best credit terms, better allowances for returned goods, free technical advice not available to periphery firms;

9) Center firms occasionally participate in joint projects barred to periphery enterprises—these may include the exchange of technological secrets, shared transportation facilities, and the community development of raw materials;

10) Center firms have significant litigation advantages—best lawyers, most thorough legal brief preparation—giving them better protection of their legal rights, sometimes enabling center firms to win out-of-court settlements because of legal and economic strength, not because of the inherent weight of their case;

11) Center firms have public relations advantages—disproportionate access to mass media, use of public opinion polls, psychological research;

12) The center has favored access to finance when credit is restricted—center firm risk is better spread and such firms have easier entry into bond and security markets;

13) Center firms have a political advantage—they can maintain a full-time staff in Washington to advise on timing, the locus of critical decision making, what information to prepare; such factors are often decisive in gaining favorable laws and administra-

tive rulings on such matters as tariffs, taxes, and subsidies, as well as successful contract bids.[22]

Nonmanufacturing Industries

OUR BRIEF SURVEY of structural types within the center and periphery economies is complete. We have said little about the government-regulated social overhead capital industries. Although perhaps one-fifth of United States national income originates in industries subject to direct regulation, prices in these sectors must pass close governmental scrutiny, while output tends to be closely attuned to fluctuations in goods production. Trade, like manufacturing, is composed of both center and periphery elements; the center is spreading in trade with periphery remnants remaining nonetheless vigorous in many areas. As for mining we should note a recent coal industry study which suggests that an important part of the largest noncenter mining industry in the United States does not differ substantially in structure from manufacturing. Professor Reed Moyer characterizes the Midwestern coal industry as one dominated by an oligopolistic core of medium to large firms surrounded by a small-firm competitive fringe.[23] Other sectors are important, but manufacturing is pivotal for it sets the rhythm for movements in output and employment in trade, transportation, communication, and mining. Labor, agriculture, and government receive extended consideration in later chapters.

The important financial sector also resembles manufacturing in structure. Postwar commercial banking is notable for (1) a strong merger movement reducing the number of independent banking units, and (2) a high degree of asset concentration. During the 1950's, 887 new banks were chartered but 1,503 banks were absorbed by merger while ninety-eight discontinued for other reasons.[24] The largest fifteen commercial banks held about

22. Most of these points are discussed in Corwin D. Edwards, "Conglomerate Bigness as a Source of Power," in George J. Stigler, (ed.), *Business Concentration and Price Policy,* Princeton University Press, 1955, pp. 331–332.
23. Reed Moyer, *Competition in the Midwestern Coal Industry,* Harvard University Press, 1964, p. 202.
24. The following data on financial institutions was taken from the U.S. House of Representatives, Committee on the Judiciary, *Interlocks in Corporate Management,* Government Printing Office, 1965, pp. 164–192.

27.3 percent of all commercial bank deposits on December 28, 1962; the ten leading mutual savings banks held approximately 23.3 percent of total deposits in such institutions on the same date. The concentration by region is dramatic. The five largest banks held over 50 percent of commercial bank deposits in every large U.S. metropolitan region in June, 1962.

As in banking, so with life insurance. The life insurance industry has undergone a pronounced postwar merger movement; in 1962, the ten largest life insurance companies controlled 61.4 percent of all life insurance assets. Financial enterprises, like their manufacturing and trade counterparts, fall into center and periphery slots. Nor is the division between financial and commercial-industrial interests unambiguous. U.S. life insurance companies invest more funds in corporate securities than in any other general asset. At the end of 1962, 43.4 percent of life insurance assets was concentrated in corporate securities, representing five times the amount of such life insurance investment at the end of World War II. Further interlocking directorates between leading insurance companies and center economy firms are widespread. Where center firm ownership is concentrated in insurance company hands, a link often remains between ownership and control.

Attitudes toward the Center Economy

GIVEN THE generic character of key industries in the center economy, it is quite easy to draw conclusions that appear correct in substance but, when translated into policy, can do the economy much long-run harm. Such reasoning might proceed as follows:

* * *

Like other industrial economies, the American economic structure takes the form of an industrial pyramid. Certain key industries, found in the manufacturing sector, play critical roles in the economy's total performance.

These key sectors are overwhelmingly dominated by the giant firms composing the center economy—firms possessing impregnable economic, political, and legal advantages. Not content to dominate key industries alone, center firms have spread their influence backward into earlier mining and manufacturing stages as well as forward into wholesale and retail trade. They are now endeavoring through conglomerate merger to reach, octopus fashion, into even still distant areas of economic activity. Several center firms are already so industrially omnifarious that their major concern is for the prosperity of the total economy, for as long as the U.S. economy is strong, they too are strong.

Just as the center economy dominates American productive capacity, the economic power elite, those relatively few men who serve as directors and managers of center firms, dominate the center economy. Important business decisions are indeed being made and these men are making them. For there is a substantial separation of corporate ownership from corporate control in such firms; holding companies and interlocking directorates solidify the center world. As a result the American economic system is led by a finite number of all too visible hands.

Although too large and heterogeneous a group to engage in active collusion, the men at the vortex think alike. They operate under a common climate of opinion which gives ideological meaning to the business establishment. In a capitalistic society where money, not government authority, controls the increasingly effective means of mass communication, public opinion and political action tend to fall under the same nexus as private production. Control of production and opinion is subtle and indirect, but it is no less effective because consumers and workers are given the mask of autonomy.

The limiting powers formerly provided through competition no longer operate in the newly emerged center economy. Periphery competitors and suppliers, and indeed the public interest, are protected by little more than the collective conscience of center firm managers. Surely the small businessman and the unorganized consumer deserve better economic guardians than a faceless business establishment freed from the harsh necessities of classical competiton. If we cannot break these center economy giants into periphery dwarfs without paying a heavy price in productive efficiency, is it not our duty to insist on more visible government control over the heart of the economic system? Should the Federal government not at least limit the future growth of center firms, confining them to their present areas of primary activity?

*   *   *

These sentiments and the issues flowing from them find superficial confirmation in the present chapter. Yet proper emphasis belongs elsewhere. Every taxonomy assumes a static cast. But industrial economies do not hold a fixed form for long. A changing technology provides a slow but continuous metamorphosis in economic structure. Today's key industries may slide down the industrial hierarchy into relative oblivion. We noticed, for instance, how the machine tool industry, once the catalyst of technological convergence, is now falling slowly under the influence of electronic automation.

The challenge of survival greatly motivates those firms close to the scientific vortex. As the rate of technological change increases, the secular decline of all markets is speeded up. New products age quickly and this fact prods the center firm to sharpen its product development and marketing processes. The center economy is, then, a place of feverish activity. Traditional markets face continual challenges from rival center firms and newly developed substitute products. The center economy competition between research departments is perhaps no less intense than that between marketing departments.

Technological Change and the Business-Industrial Structure

OUR FOUR pivotal concepts—technical production structure, key industries, center economy, and periphery economy—are all dynamic, intertwined in a mutually reinforcing pattern of continuing evolution. Manufacturing has moved from a handicraft, small batch orientation toward major continuous flow output complemented by a rejuvenated small batch sector supplying custom inputs. Key industries are far from fixed. As an industrial economy matures, its economic structure becomes more complex. Our key industry list for the late 1960's and early 1970's is possibly larger than a comparable list for the 1920's would have been. And by the year 2000, the list will perhaps be larger still. Old key industries, like steel and machine tools, may retain their critical status, but they are joined by new industries as technology surges through, then beyond, them.

At the turn of the century, when the center economy was first spreading its domain over the early key industries where it originated, a corresponding wave of antibig business sentiment is easy to understand. To the vision of a single generation, the heart of the American industrial system seemed forever caught in the grasp of a few tycoons. Yet while key industries have increased in number, center firms have expanded their interests into an enormous variety of new fields, many of them unrelated to the firm's industrial beginnings. Indeed, the drift of the future seems to be moving toward pure conglomerates, center firms having no industrial base whatsoever.

In the midst of such dramatic change, the periphery economy seems relatively stable. It existed before American industrialization in the 1840's, and in some respects it follows the same economic rhythm today. But the periphery economy, once industrialization takes hold, becomes in part an appendage of the dynamic center. Caught in the undertow of relentless technical and organizational transformation, periphery enterprises cannot but follow in their several ways the paths pioneered by the center economy. Relatively small-scale they may remain, followers of trends set elsewhere, but stagnate they cannot in the face of an ever-changing environment.

The periphery economy still embodies much of the stern discipline of classical competition. The actions of every individual entrepreneur are circumscribed by market forces beyond his control. In the center economy such is clearly not the case. Where oligopoly is the dominant competitive condition, the sting of competitor retaliation becomes too certain and too great. An uneasy but potentially stable pricing peace emerges; when market disruption can be total, neither individual firms nor the public interest is served by continual price war.

So it is that the contemporary antitrusters find themselves on the horns of an enforcement dilemma. If they fragment center firms, they may restore classical competition, but consequently economies of scale and technological progress may suffer. To get an industry structure favorable to vigorous price competition would require dramatic legal action, the dissection of major business enterprises. Such a forceful act by the courts would surely unsettle the business community and private investment would likely suffer from it. Even if the transitition to a more competitive economy proved short-lived, it could exact a heavy toll in lost output. If we admit that we cannot tear the center asunder without suffering a decline in economic welfare, we are allowing the directors of the center economy to control the nation's economic muscle without submitting them to the discipline of the classical marketplace or the democratic ballot box. If defenders of the new masters of management assure us they are "responsible" men, surely we can ask, "Responsible to whom?"

But here again reformers, and a considerable number of professional economists, subject themselves to misplaced apprehension. The underlying structural changes are real and profound, but the controversy over appropriate economic policy is couched in the limiting reference of an inadequate economic theory. For too long we have forced a single theoretical construction to explain the workings of two economies. The economist's theory of the firm fits the periphery economy quite well. It fits the center economy hardly at all. Unfortunately we have all, professional and layman alike, been prone to condemn, not the overextended theory, but the center economy. Viewed in price-competition terms, the center economy cannot but perform poorly. The two disparate economic arenas are continually judged by this single standard, one refined by Alfred Marshall just at the time when the center economy was beginning to form.

So the center economy leads a furtive intellectual existence. Reasonably efficient and immensely productive, it has never been able to throw off the shadow of monopoly. Lacking a theoretical structure to explain their functional place, center managers are forced to defend their enterprises in the language of Adam Smith. Lacking a present-day theoretical justification, prophets of the center must cloak their message in the rationalizations of the late eighteenth century.

Perhaps a new view of the role of the economic center should begin by stressing center firm imperatives. Center firms must follow the new technology, else they fall into the Marshallian trap. They must continually move where technology flourishes, picking up new firms and products as they discard the old. Progress is indeed their most important product as well as their most stringent taskmaster. Center firms survive in the very long run only when they leave established short-run positions for the challenge of new products and new industries. Thus the static, short-run analysis of conventional price theory cannot catch and effectively evaluate the long-run dynamism of the center. Freed of the rigors of short-run competition, center firms must henceforth use this freedom relentlessly to pursue the technological fountain of youth. The foolish center firms who ignore this lesson may revel in monopoly profit for a season, but their day of reckoning will surely come. Technology provides in the long run no less of a mortal threat for center firms than competition provides for periphery firms in the here and now.

A viable microeconomics of the total economy must begin with a clear and rigorous definition of periphery and center firms, stressing the ways in which they differ. To this task we now turn.

5. The Economics of the Periphery Firm

THE U.S. economy embraces two economic systems. Composed of small firms the periphery economy has the longest history but is now the less important. The center economy is rooted in key manufacturing industries and mass retailing. Here large firms predominate. Yet the business population cannot be easily divided into large firms and small. In both economies the extreme cases are perspicuous; members of the industrial high command such as General Motors, General Dynamics, and General Electric represent center firms, while the independent business with less than ten employees can only reside in the periphery. But where to draw the line? What of the multitude in the middle?

Perhaps sociological distinctions between the two economies are reasonably clear. While statistical definitions, based on number of employees, total assets, or yearly sales yield a sizable middle class of firms, in terms of economic power, self-image, and style of operation, the overwhelming majority belong to either the expansive center of economic affairs or the traditional periphery economy. Power, image, style—however intangible these terms, they do describe very real phenomena in the field of investigations social scientists call their own. A satisfactory measure for power is elusive, yet business firms either do, or they do not, have significant influence over and knowlege of the major technical, political, and economic forces that determine their life chances. Business images are difficult to describe, but even courts of law recognize "good will" and similar unseen assets. Such a line of social demarcation resembles a wide gray stroke, not a thin black one, but the fundamental distinction between great and small nations, churches, and business enterprises is commonly used and is uncommonly useful.

But neither economists nor policymakers find sociological definitions wholly satisfactory. Given a legislative mandate to aid small business, the Small Business Administration (SBA) resorts to numerical criteria to define its flock. For manufacturing concerns, depending on the industry, 250 to 1,000 employee boundaries are used. In classifying wholesalers as small business, the SBA uses annual sales of $5 million or less; for construction firms, $7.5 million. Annual sales of $1 million or less qualify general retailers for SBA help; $2 million, most grocers, and $1 million, the majority of service enterprises. Under these definitions, about 95 percent of American business firms fit into the small business category.

Such definitions are strict enough, but they, too, are unsatisfactory for economic analysis. They gloss over the crucial differences in structure and economic function discussed at some length in the last chapter. Our definition will be constructed on the analytically rigorous foundation of the theory of supply and demand.

Demand and Supply in Brief

THE DEMAND SIDE of this familiar dichotomy can be stated quite simply. Consumer incomes are limited, while wants are insatiable. Consumers must therefore ration their expenditures on any one product, for the purchase of any given good or service restricts the ability to consume everything else. In general, consumers will purchase more of a commodity when its price is low, less when it is high. A low price allows buyers to purchase additional quantities of the product in question as well as more of other products if they so desire. Thus, for most goods, movements in price and quantity purchased will be inversely related. The theoretical underpinnings of demand theory are complicated and difficult to reveal, but the basic principle appeals to common experience. If prices are high, consumers will in most cases buy less; when they are low, assuming incomes constant, more will be purchased.

The principles of supply are more complicated. Business firms must sell their output at a price that covers their costs and allows some margin for profit. Profit fills the gap between cost and revenue; profit per unit of output is the difference between unit costs and unit revenue. Since all business firms are vitally interested in their profit levels, the most important elements in supply analysis are these two determinants of profits—costs and revenue. The branch of economic analysis that relates these critical variables is known as the theory of the firm.

We shall begin with costs. What firms must buy to produce an output are called factors of production. They are traditionally categorized as land (including raw materials), labor, capital, and management. These are sometimes called factor inputs. As production increases, cost per unit of output inevitably falls for a time. This is true at low levels of operation because most of the factors are indivisible. All of these parts must be assembled to produce a single unit of output; if but one unit is produced, the total cost of the entire operation must be assigned to that single unit. In most cases the production of the second unit will be virtually costless, for the productive factors are already assembled but idle. Thus the second unit's production is likely to cut per unit costs in half; the production of a third unit will split constant total costs roughly three ways.

Consequently marginal costs, the cost of producing the last unit, fall very rapidly as production increases at low levels, but begin to fall more slowly as the factors arrive at productive capacity. In the short run, defined as a period of time so short that plant capacity cannot be augmented, marginal costs begin to rise after a time. This is true because the most efficient level of production, where the average cost per unit is lowest, does not exactly coincide with the plant's maximum output. It is usually possible to produce additional output with a given plant beyond the most efficient level of output, but when physical output is maximized, per unit costs rise quickly.

In brief, marginal costs fall rapidly at first as the factors of production are more fully employed, then less rapidly as factor productivity reaches peak efficiency. In the short run, marginal costs eventually reach a trough as production expands. The least-cost point represents that place in production where factors work at maximum efficiency. The plant can produce additional output, but it does so by overextending the available factors and thus increasing marginal costs. If we depict graphically the fall and then rise of marginal costs as output expands in the short run, our cost curve resembles the letter "U." Economists commonly refer to such cost behavior as a U-shaped cost curve.

The behavior of the firm's revenue is somewhat less involved. The shape of the revenue curve analogous to the cost curve is determined by the type of market in which the firm operates. Markets are divided into four types—perfect competition, monopolistic competition, oligopoly, and monopoly. In a perfectly competitive market, the portion of total industry production carried on in any one firm is so small it has no influence on total industry supply or price. Thus the last item produced can be sold for the same price as the first item. All firms in such markets are pricetakers; small and competitively weak they cannot sell their product at a price above the going price. In the other three market types, individual firms are large enough in relation to their market to exert some influence on both total industry supply and price. The influence of specific firms is substantial under monopolistic competition, greater under oligopoly, and total in cases of monopoly. In every market structure except perfect competition, assuming a constant demand, additional firm outputs must be sold at a lower price.

Combining marginal revenue and marginal costs, we see that the cost of producing an additional unit falls to a trough and then rises, while the revenue to be gained from an additional unit's sale either remains constant throughout the range of possible production (perfect competition) or falls as production expands. Thus, in the short-run, businessmen will find one level of output, and only one, where the rising cost of producing additional output equals the constant or falling revenue to be gained from its sale. At this output total profit is maximized.

If the firm produces any units beyond this point, the cost of producing these units will exceed their selling price. If the firm produces less units, it forgoes the additions to total profits that can be gained as long as marginal costs are less than marginal revenue.

An increase in marginal revenue, or a decrease in marginal costs, should, other things being equal, induce profit maximizing firms to increase their output and hence their profit. Unlike demand, the quantity supplied and the going price of an item are directly related. A higher price will call forth additional production. The market is stable when the going price is one that induces firms to produce just the quantity of a good that consumers wish to purchase at that price.

The above sketch bluntly outlines the contemporary theory of supply and demand. There is probably more dissatisfaction among economists with the supply portion and the underlying theory of the firm than with any other branch of formal doctrine. That the theory deals with matters of vital importance is beyond dispute. It isolates and projects generalizations about such crucial economic data as costs, revenue, output, and price; by making essential analytical distinctions, differentiating between average and marginal units, variable and fixed costs, its technical terms contribute a ponderous but meaningful vocabulary to the entire economic lexicon. The economic terrain surveyed by the theory of the firm is so strategic that even if the theory were totally useless, as it certainly is not, economists would still be forced to reckon with the problems it poses, undoubtedly searching for concepts similar to those the theory employs.

Whatever its shortcomings, the presently modeled theory of the firm performs one critical task reasonably well. The division of market structures into perfect competition, monopolistic competition, oligopoly, and monopoly provides a viable taxonomy of horizontal firm relationships. The four conventional market types and their accompanying analytical constructs set forth with considerable precision the common price and output strategies used by several firms occupying identical markets. Such classification and analysis proves indispensable. The interaction among firms within a given industry is perhaps the most important set of interfirm relations in the economic system.

Flaws in the Theory of the Firm

USEFUL AS IT IS, the current theory of industrial organization has two unfortunate blemishes. First, since the market provides the theory's frame of reference, and since the term "market," as commonly used in firm theory, refers only to a specific product and its close substitutes, the hypothetical "firm" of the theory corresponds to real life enterprises only if existing business establishments either (1) produce only one commodity and/or its close substitutes or (2) multiproduct firms manage the pricing and output of each product *as if* it were unrelated to all other firm products. In manufacturing, the first condition is not unknown. Many firms do specialize in a single product, or in a group of closely related products; but these are typically the smaller, less important firms of the periphery economy. For large, diversified firms, the second condition cannot occur. Where managerial and other overhead costs form a significant portion of total cost, diversified firms cannot know what costs would be if they produced a single product. Because of important joint costs and the arbitrary nature of cost allocation, firms seldom segregate costs and profits on a market by market basis. When such separation is performed, managers have little confidence in it. *Thus in markets populated with multiproduct firms, the "theory of the firm" is in fact only a "theory of the product."* It does not describe the activities of the firm falling outside the market under analysis, nor does it take into account the effect these other activities exert on the production and marketing of the product in question.

The second shortcoming is equally damaging when the theory of the firm is used to analyze the center economy. The theory in essence only applies to the short run. *There is no long-run theory of the firm, or to put it differently, the long run is assumed to be nothing more than a series of consecutive short runs.* The "long-run" average cost curve provides an excellent illustration. Since the short run is defined as a time period so short that additional plant capacity cannot be obtained, the long run is a period sufficient in length to admit all possible changes in capacity. Thus the firm can build any size plant it desires in the long run. Short-run curves being U-shaped, long-run curves are shown graphically by drawing a series of overlapping U-shaped curves with troughs that fall and then rise as their respective capacities increase. The long-run average cost curve is then drawn so that it is tangent to all of the short-run curves. Often called an "envelope" curve, it is made up of small segments of the various short-run curves. The long-run curve has no meaning apart from the short-run curves.[1] Figure 5-1 shows a family of

FIGURE 5–1

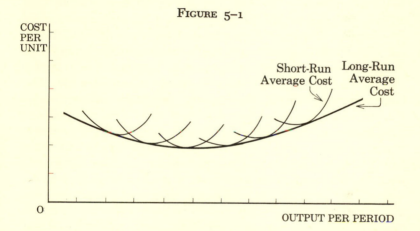

short-run average cost curves enclosed by a traditional long-run average cost curve. Each individual short-run curve represents a specific plant size. The plant whose short-run trough is tangent with the trough of the long-run curve is the most efficient plant providing that the firm's demand allows such a plant to operate at its least-cost output. The short-run curves turn up because at some output their plant facilities are overutilized. Long-run curves ascend only because economists assume that beyond

1. A good, technical discussion of the long-run cost curve's dependence on short-run cost curves can be found in H. H. Liebhafsky, *The Nature of Price Theory*, The Dorsey Press, Inc., 1963, pp. 179–180.

some output level the efficiency of management will fall, boosting average costs by more than they are deflated by scale economies accruing to other factors.

A Definition of the Periphery Firm

FROM THESE two analytical faults in the theory of the firm—the failure to encompass multiproduct firms and the lack of a genuine long-run theory—we shall develop our center and periphery firm definitions. Periphery firms conform rather closely to the traditional textbook descriptions of firm behavior. Besides their propensity to produce a single line of goods, small periphery firms are forced to assume an exclusively short-run attitude.

The periphery is populated by firms which cannot, given their present size and structure, achieve potentially limitless long-run growth. When their productive capacity increases beyond some level, long-run average costs *necessarily rise*. With a heavy reliance on local sources of factor supply (including management), their range of production technique is severely limited; their factor supply curves tend to be more inelastic than those confronting their larger center economy counterparts. In many cases they own technically inferior equipment. They are relatively poor credit risks, more dependent on local credit sources, less able to depend on internal financing. Security markets are often too expensive for their use. Periphery entrepreneurs have a lower average level of education, yet management decisions are more dependent on a single individual, reflecting his limitations and mistakes. Expansion is usually dependent on local market growth, but when the local market grows too rapidly, the possibility of center firm invasion increases.

When the small firm has good growth potential, it must usually borrow to realize such advantage. Yet if, as growth continues, more is borrowed than reinvested from past profits, there is increasing danger that an unexpected reversal of economic fortunes may leave the value of the firm's assets below its liabilities. One solution lies in "noncontractual" borrowing, but this stipulates the sharing of ownership and control. The periphery business that undergoes rapid growth must soon assume much of the center form. With such expansion the firm's internal structure must eventually be reshaped to resemble the diversified and decentralized cast assumed by the members of the center economy. [NORMAN E. HATHAWAY, President, Velsicol Chemical Corporation — *It's a matter of scale. A company reaches a certain size, and it just can't go on doing business in the same old way.*] [2] To achieve unlimited life, and consequently a long-run perspective, periphery firms can only outgrow the periphery economy. Edith Penrose puts it well: "There is considerable evidence that small firms, because of their size, are restricted by their environment to certain types of opportunity where the prospects of continued expansion are extremely limited." [3]

The defining quality of periphery firms is settled by *small size* and *limited potential.* Conversely, the center economy is composed of firms combining *large size* and *unlimited potential.* The threshold separating the two economies is a no man's land for finance and management. A firm striving to move into the center economy unaided must go through three distinct financing phases. In the beginning financial problems revolve around seed capital. The managers of the new enterprise seek money to start operations. If the enterprise succeeds, expansion may carry them into the nebulous threshold region where the firm ceases to be a pure periphery enterprise but is not yet a member of the center. It is this threshold phase that proves fatal for many successful periphery concerns. Financial requirements are too large for noncommercial sources, but the firm is still sequestered from the center financial community. For the fortunate few firms which can, in time, emerge from the valley of corporate disintegration, the third phase of public stock and bond offerings, center commercial bank access, and accumulating internal liquidity provide a welcome financial haven. When these become available, the fortunate business pilgrim has entered the center economy.

Managerial pitfalls threatening the ambitious firm's ascent out of the periphery seem no less menacing. In the periphery

2. *Forbes,* Vol. 98, No. 8 (October 15, 1966), p. 33.
3. Edith Penrose, *The Theory of the Growth of the Firm,* Basil Blackwell & Mott, Ltd., 1959, p. 215.

economy, firms adhere to a family life style. The founder or founders governs the successful periphery enterprise in much the same way as a wise, tolerant, resourceful head of household manages family affairs. But once the firm expands into the managerial twilight zone, the threshold between periphery and center, the corporation must undergo reorganization. Dispersed and delegated, management responsibility is still coordinated at the top. Operating routine is closely supervised, but it must not crowd out long-term planning. Traditional products must be produced and marketed efficiently to yield satisfactory profits, yet this yield from conventional sources must now be devoted in part to exploring new avenues of firm growth. The firm which functions well in the periphery economy, then without fatal mishaps crosses the dividing threshold, may emerge with a transformed financial and managerial structure suited to center economy operations. Such a firm is indeed a business bird of rare feather. This straight road up from the periphery and into the center is so long and torturous, so littered with obstacles, it is no wonder that few have the courage to attempt it. Those who do are a monument to the tenacity of the rugged enterprising spirit in America. [HARRY E. SINGLETON, Chairman and President, Teledyne, Inc.— *GM, AT&T, U.S. Steel, DuPont—I want to build a company of that type.*] [From *Forbes* magazine— *Now Teledyne is at a dangerous point. No longer a small company, it is not yet a big one.*] [4]

The overwhelming majority of small periphery firms desires neither to grow into the center economy nor to compete with it. They are engaged in subcenter competitive and routine business operations. Competitive because the barriers to entry are usually low. Routine because they follow conventional periphery managerial techniques; they rely on tested methods of producing and distribute long-accepted products. These characteristic periphery enterprises may be free agents, filling the interstices of the industrial system without major center economy intrusion as a factor supplier or product buyer. Or they may be satellites, deriving their revenue either from subcontracting or providing services or materials for center firms, or from distributing the center firm's output.

Manufacturing free agents produce jewelry, games and toys, signs and advertising displays, and the like. Distributing free agents are so common that they need no illustration. Many exist in the sheltered markets of small towns or in the slums of large cities.[5] Machine tool firms are usually backward satellites, while perhaps the most familiar forward satellites are gasoline service stations and automobile dealerships.

The third periphery category, the loyal opposition, includes two fairly distinct firm types. One type is a *pioneering* small firm, operating in an industry dominated by the center. Well-known in the electronics field, the pioneering firm often develops and introduces a new product or process simulating a center-produced commodity. The ideas may even have been developed in but never marketed by a center firm. [ROBERT L. KIRBY, Industrial Products Group Vice-President, Westinghouse — *We've always had good manufacturing, good talent, good products, good people, great research. Yet no one has ever been able to get everything working together. You wouldn't believe the long list of product discoveries which have come out of our labs, never to be heard of until a competitor made a success of them years later.*][6]

Entrepreneurs founding pioneering loyal opposition firms may come from the offices or labs of established center firms, bringing with them the benefits of center economy know-how. Or they may come from the universities, particularly from the physical science departments, where scientists hunger to turn a laboratory discovery into a financial windfall. These technically sophisticated periphery firms are predictably single-product firms, and therein lies their commercial peril. [KENNETH J. GERMESHAUSEN, Chairman, EG&G, Inc. — *Too many engineers build a new company around a single excellent product. They fail to realize that the life of any product is limited, and you must have something ready to take its place.*][7] Pioneering loyal

5. The "sheltering" effect of urban slums on small retailers is documented in Basil Zimmer, *Rebuilding Cities: The Effects of Displacement and Relocation on Small Business,* Quadrangle Books, 1964; and David Caplovitz, *The Poor Pay More,* The Free Press of Glencoe, 1963.

6. *Forbes,* Vol. 95, No. 11 (June 1, 1965), p. 26.

7. *Forbes,* Vol. 97, No. 11 (June 1, 1966), p. 70.

opposition firms are also notoriously deficient in merchandising experience, an often fatal weakness in markets blanketed by center firm expertise.

A second group of loyal opposition firms challenges center firms in their strong markets without relying on pioneering. The American economy is so large and affluent that there is often room for well-run periphery firms marketing a single line of center-dominated products nationally or serving a large regional market in competition with more remote center competitors.

Center firm competitive advantages rest basically upon two types of scale economies—one with technical, the other with organizational, origins. Potential technical economies of scale exist when the most efficient technology allows output to expand more rapidly than the increase in equiproportionate factor inputs. This occurs many times in industries having continuous flow production possibilities, such as automobiles, petroleum, steel, aluminum, and household detergents. When the price in these industries is maintained well *above* the costs of the most efficient center plant, independent periphery enterprises may be able to operate, as they do in petroleum, quite effectively. If center firms have been slow in adopting the new continuous flow production, as in steel, periphery firm costs may equal or even fall below those in the center. But so long as technical economies exist, periphery firms in the industry live a precarious existence.

When the continuous flow technology is adopted, and should industry prices closely reflect unit costs, small-scale periphery firms can be forced from the field without antitrust violations. In industries subject to radical fluctuations in output, it may pay to put only that capacity necessary for fulfilling the nation's minimum demands on a continuous flow basis, leaving considerable plant capacity in the large batch category. At full employment, periphery firms can still compete even with center firms utilizing all their technical economies; but if full employment is a sometime thing, how can the loyal opposition periphery survive recession? During business lulls, the loyal opposition depends on "paternal pricing" by technically superior center firms.

Organizational economies of scale prevail among center firms and, thus, represent a more general periphery firm threat. These economies include a more effective utilization of specialized personnel, reduced financing costs, increased advertising effectiveness per dollar spent, and better distributor organization and financing. Yet the U.S. economy remains extensive enough to give many scale economies to small firms specializing in a single strand of a diversified center firm product line, especially when the economy operates near full employment. Where technical economies are not prohibitive, or when they are not fully used, organizational economies will not completely bar loyal opposition competition.

One excellent example of a sturdy loyal opposition firm surviving in a center-dominated market is the Maytag Company of Newton, Iowa. Maytag makes only two products, washers and dryers. Comparatively a small firm in its industry (about $124 million in yearly sales), it produces machines which compete with such volume producers as Whirlpool (a Sears satellite), General Electric, Borg-Warner, General Motors, American Motors, and Ford. Even so, Maytag captures about 10 percent of the market. [EMERSON HIGDON, President, Maytag—*We are a short-line specialized producer dealing only in laundry equipment. Everything we do is keyed to this: our tightly controlled distribution through factory-owned branches; our policy of not going in for annual model changes or special models. Everything is keyed to specialization.*] [8]

A prominent loyal opposition firm in the steel industry is the Granite City Steel Company of Granite City, Illinois, just across the Mississippi River from St. Louis. Granite City Steel supplies a large urban market partially sheltered from the Pittsburgh-based center producers 620 miles away. But reduced transportation costs, center steel firm expansion, and new steel technology now pose a serious competitive threat to Granite City's local monopoly status. Nor is it yet clear what long-run effect the government's active interest in paternal pricing will have on the loyal opposition in steel. The loyal opposition may have been nurtured solely by big steel's competitive lethargy, technical tardiness, and monopoly pricing.

8. *Forbes*, Vol. 95, No. 7 (April 1, 1965), p. 17.

If a sheltered-market periphery firm, like Granite City Steel, tries to expand, it will incur a falling marginal revenue if sales growth does not occur in its immediate geographic area; this happens because of transportation costs. Even if the price paid by the buyer remains constant, the addition of higher transportation charges will lower the marginal revenue to the firm. Where transportation costs are a significant part of price, as they are in steel, marginal revenue to the firm falls when they rise. Sheltered-market periphery firms are, consequently, confined to a limited geographic market; but if their local market grows significantly it is certain to attract center firms, meaning possible center invasion.

The loyal opposition thrives on center firm managerial omission and often exists by center firm pricing permission. Center firms may find it more profitable to devote their talent and money to new fields than to soak up the last bits of any one market; or center firms may grow complacent under reasonable profits without aggressively pursuing either new cost reducing technology or scattered markets. A too aggressive center firm can stir up antitrust trouble; paternal pricing preserves comfortable center firm profits (when prices are uniform throughout the industry) while protecting loyal opposition firms so as to be buffered against government prosecution.

Satellite firms are tied to the center in more tangible ways. Center firm satellite ownership is not uncommon, but by far the most prevalent form of center-satellite tie is financial. The largest volume of funds for small retail firms comes not from conventional lenders and investors, but from selling transactions between periphery distributors and large manufacturers and wholesalers. The most common type of center-satellite credit is "open-book" or "accounts receivable" credit, arising from a practice of billing permitting a number of days to pass before payment is demanded. The smaller the periphery firm, the greater its reliance upon such trade credit. Since changes in trade credit terms are not well-publicized, they pave a subtle avenue for center firm competition.

Making cash loans and guaranteeing the credit of both backward and forward satellites also signal center firms' patronage.

New equipment is sometimes provided satellites or financed for them by sponsoring center firms. Such center firm aid can be invaluable to a small satellite firm, particularly in times of credit stringency, for satellites must rely heavily on outside financing despite their ordinarily low credit ratings. Center firms may also use their preferred access to money in the creation of satellites. [VIRGIL BOYD, Vice-President, Chrysler, referring to the Chrysler Dealers Enterprise Program — *What we generally do through the program is put up about 75% of the $200,000 or so to set up an average dealership.*] [9] In many industries center firms extend the hand of credit through the distributor to the customer, binding both with credit ties. [WILLIAM A. HEWITT, President, Deere and Company — *A satisfactory volume of machinery sales to farmers requires that there be a ready supply of credit to finance those sales. Machinery manufacturers learned this by hard experience. To us, credit is a sales tool.*] [10] This customer credit is available through center manufacturers and center retailers for the purchase of a wide variety of merchandise. Readily available center credit assures center firms and their satellites of a flexible financial system unavailable to the loyal opposition and free agents. [11]

Outside manufacturing and retailing, periphery-type business organizations are often coordinated by strong unions. Unions have considerable coordinating power in construction, newspapers, public utilities, and local transit because of large lumps of employment, limited possibility of new firm entry, and low industry mobility. [12] Construction provides a near-perfect example of a nonmanufacturing, periphery-oriented sector. Each year sees some 8,000 negotiations between highly autonomous local construction unions, loosely organized into eighteen building trades, with thousands of small and medium-size contractors.

9. *Forbes*, Vol. 96, No. 6 (September 15, 1965), p. 23.

10. Quoted in U.S. Board of Governors, Federal Reserve System, *Financing Small Business*, U.S. Government Printing Office, 1958, p. 364. This collection of expert opinion on small business finance is an invaluable reference for anyone interested in credit sources available to the periphery economy.

11. For a study of sixty-nine finance companies owned by center firms, including Sears, GE, GM, Ford, ACF, and International Harvester, see Paul H. Banner, "Competition, Credit Policy, and the Captive Finance Company," *Quarterly Journal of Economics*, Vol. LXXII, No. 2 (May, 1958), pp. 241–258.

12. Martin Segal, "The Relation Between Union Wage Impact and Market Structure," *Quarterly Journal of Economics*, Vol. LXXVIII, No. 1 (February, 1964), pp. 96–114.

When labor costs rise simultaneously for all contractors in an area, job bids tend to increase uniformly. Where unions coordinate their demands in a market area, no single employer is penalized competitively for a high settlement. In addition to coordinated area demands by specific construction locals, contractors are also susceptible to a wage ratchet effect; a generous settlement with the bricklayers encourages the carpenters, hod carriers, painters, plumbers, and sheet metal workers to ask for more. Consequently, on-site picketing means that when one local strikes, other union members usually honor the picket lines, refusing to work. Construction jobs are complementary, so that one craft often cannot work until another has finished, making strikes effective even when other crafts *are* willing to work.

Unions manage a measure of unity in periphery-type industries and, outside manufacturing, their contributions to market coordination are often considerable. But union coordination is basically limited to securing short-run gains for workers. What unions, with their craft orientation, cannot provide is technological flexibility, an attribute central to progressive center firms. The lack of center-style organization in construction, an industry employing more than 4 million workers, is a matter of serious government concern. [THE COUNCIL OF ECONOMIC ADVISERS — *The inflationary cost and price situations in the (construction) industry reflect to some extent its prosperity, especially in its industrial and commercial sectors. They also suggest the existence of more permanent structural problems which should be of vital concern for both the industry and the community at large. There have been important technological changes in various sectors of the industry, but the total technical progress is clearly insufficient.*] [13]

The Machine Tool Industry: A Case Study

A BRIEF CASE STUDY of an industry dominated by periphery enterprise will help, perhaps, to dramatize the periphery

---

13. *Economic Report of the President*, U.S. Government Printing Office, January, 1966, pp. 85–86.

economy's salient characteristics. Machine tools is a key industry, an indispensable part of any fully integrated industrial complex. It is a *regenerative* industry, composed on the technical level of machines that make other machines, *including* other machine tools. With chemicals and electronics, machine tools compose the economy's reproductive capacity. Having machine tools, a domestic economy can, through time, reproduce itself; without them, it cannot.

During the nineteenth century, machine tools was a locus for technical convergence, an innovational seedbed. This is no longer true. Machine tool firms have produced no major technological breakthrough in the last generation. There have, to be sure, been changes. Machine tool speed has increased sharply, but much of this progress has been frittered away through idle machine time. Machine tools have been standardized along with replacement parts, but the impetus for standardization came from large customers, primarily the automobile industry. Two major innovations are now spreading throughout machine tool firms—carbide tools with their related technology, and numerical controls; both, however, originated outside the industry. The first is a foreign import, the second was developed by government-sponsored research in the aerospace industry.[14]

Such an internal technological quietus in the machine tool industry typifies long-run problems facing the periphery. It explains, in part, why such a critical industry remains outside the center economy. Historical circumstance also hinders the industry. A mainstay of industrialization, the industry is quite old, taking part in the first industrial revolution. Machine tools, retaining its unit and small batch orientation, supports the newer mass production industries where the center economy grew up, but has never emulated, except in a few, very recent cases, their productive style. In addition, the machine tool industry has felt the burden of a classic derived demand market. The auto industry is the most important consumer of machine tool output, accounting for about 40 percent of total sales. The industry is its own second-best customer for cutting tools; the

14. For a good, brief study of the machine tool industry and technical change, see U.S. Senate, Select Committee on Small Business, *The Role and Effect of Technology in the Nation's Economy*, Part V, 88th Congress, 1st Session, 1964, pp. 579–600.

aerospace industry ranks third in sales importance. Primary dependence on these cyclically sensitive customers makes machine tools a highly growth-oriented industry, overrun with orders during a boom but severely depressed during a recession. The more stable replacement business contributes only about 10 to 15 percent of sales. For this reason alone, center firms find other investment outlets more conducive to their long-run goals.

The industry is composed of over 600 firms; the bulk of them are small enterprises. Only a handful rank as medium-size manufacturing firms or divisions of center firms—Cincinnati Milling, Warner and Swasey, American Steel Foundries, Baldwin-Lima-Hamilton (a division of Armour), Ex-Cell-O, Sunstrand, Colt Industries (Pratt and Whitney Machine Tool Division). Only a half dozen or so do any appreciable research and development; Cincinnati Milling, with a technical staff of about 300, is an industry leader. [15] Federal defense and space programs, besides serving as a major market for machine tools, support most research and development in the entire metal-forming area.

Like other periphery industries, technical change in machine tools from within is limited to the slow, evolutionary improvement of traditional products and processes. Technological innovations with major economic significance spring primarily from (1) foreign technology, (2) independent inventions, (3) new pioneering firms, (4) the invasion of traditional markets by technically advanced, established firms in other industries. Technical disruption comes to periphery industries by invasion, with the assault taking three shapes:

(1) The periphery industry borrows technology from a new industry (electronics in the case of machine tools), although the new industry remains apart.

(2) The new industry enters periphery markets, either by supplying new components, materials, or equipment (as the chemical industry supplied synthetics to textiles) or by producing peri-

---

15. It is interesting to note that comparatively large Cincinnati Milling is also a leader in diversification. Their Carlisle division manufactures a wide range of chemical additives for products ranging from paints to ice cream; Cincinnati Milling plastic circuit boards are sold to electronics firms. In addition, their overseas operations account for 25 percent of sales. See *Forbes*, Vol. 98, No. 11 (December 1, 1966), p. 30.

phery industry products (the aerospace industry manufactures numerically controlled machine tools).

(3) The new industry creates a new process or product to displace a periphery product, filling a traditional demand in a new way. Machined metal is being partially replaced by precision casting; basic metals are being superceded by plastics.

The machine tool industry, like other areas of periphery manufacturing, is under attack from several directions. During the postwar period massive government funds concentrated in a few technically advanced industrial areas—chemistry, electronics, aerospace—have exerted pressures by making new demands, presenting models of technical progress, and exploiting opportunities in traditional periphery areas. Foreign competition from European and Japanese firms has increased, while in the Detroit area, independent tool-and-die shops have been replaced by captive shops operated by center auto firms.

In general, periphery machine tool firms are ill-equipped to meet this new center challenge. They are directed toward a craft rather than a science-based technology; most are below the critical size for substantial research and innovation; the managerial focus centers on traditional production with its commitment to present methods and machines; the protection of these commitments is reinforced by powerful social sanctions— union, locality, industry, tradition. The fragmentation of the production process between many firms has resulted in no periphery firm with enough incentive to embrace radical changes, changes that might affect the whole process; no one firm in the periphery machine tool sector sees the whole productive process as a system. The organizational network was built around traditional technology, constructing a social hierarchy tied to that technology. This periphery network, both its management and labor, now resists changes in its small-scale world.

For machine tools, the center-inspired changes have arrived. These innovations are reaching out to all metal-working industries. A few metal-working firms may be large enough, or may become large enough, to utilize center techniques. The Fairfield Manufacturing Company of Lafayette, Indiana, now controls its 1,000 machine tools with an IBM computer. The typical job-shop pattern of bottlenecks, idle machines, and heavy overtime are disappearing at Fairfield, allowing great numbers of small orders to be handled in continuous assembly line fashion. Virgil G. Drake, Fairfield President, reports that the cost of the computer has been saved through cutting overtime alone. [16]

Other periphery machine and job shops may salvage a remnant of their autonomy by affiliating with a management broker. The Manufacturing and Machining Services Corporation is one such middleman, bringing together manufacturers who need metal cut, formed, or turned and shops with the capacity for such work. M&M shops guarantee a given number of machine-time hours each month, in return for access to major contracts, advertising, warehousing, low-cost transportation, cost analysis, and uniform estimating procedures. These are indications that center managerial techniques can be bought without forfeiting small-scale family ownership. [GEORGE D. KAPLAN, President, Manufacturing and Machining Services — *We act as prime contractors, making estimates, arranging for materials, finding available machine time, financing the job, paying the shop. At the same time, we assure the manufacturers of a stable source of supply, dependable quality, and accurate job estimates.*] [17]

Whatever the future of periphery metalworking, periphery prospects are dim in manufacturing generally. Between 1956 and 1963, the *Fortune* 500 top industrial firms increased their sales by 33 percent, a healthy $60 billion. While manufacturing jobs nationwide dropped 1 percent, these center economy elite raised their total by 11 percent. Meanwhile, small periphery manufacturers ($5 million or less in assets) fared progressively worse than their largest rivals (manufacturing firms with assets of $250 million or more). The small firms' sales grew only one-third as fast as the giants; small firm investment grew only 41 percent as rapidly as the giants; small firms' cash flow increased by only 4 percent (to $4 billion), while the giants boosted their cash flow by 56 percent (to $20 billion); small

16. *Business Week*, No. 1909 (April 2, 1966), p. 61.
17. *Business Week*, No. 1919 (June 11, 1966), p. 171.

firms' profits *declined* (after taxes) while the giant firms *increased* profits by 47 percent.[18]

Center Firm Encroachment on the Periphery

THE periphery-organized machine tool industry is being disrupted by center-inspired technology, but other periphery sectors are falling under center influence for other reasons. The periphery-styled construction industry is an important customer for center merchandise; thus center firms are moving into construction seeking *captive markets*. General Electric, attracted by the growth of urban renewal, has assumed 100 percent ownership of the Red Rock Hill housing project in San Francisco and a 50 percent interest in the West Haven, Connecticut, redevelopment program. Alcoa and Reynolds sell architectural aluminum to themselves by owning urban developments. Major Alcoa-owned real estate projects are located in New York (four), Pittsburgh, (two), Los Angeles, Indianapolis, Philadelphia, and San Francisco. [LEON E. HICKMAN, Executive Vice-President, Alcoa — *Urban redevelopment is good for Alcoa, and Alcoa is good for urban redevelopment.*] [19]

Many center firms are attracted to the periphery in their quest for *distribution efficiency*. Satisfactory distribution can often be achieved through dealer satellites, as in petroleum and automobiles. And center firm marketing control can also be maintained by establishing an impregnable market franchise system reinforced by "pull-through" advertising. Monsanto, the third largest U.S. chemical firm, has licensed Chemstrand, a synthetic fiber, to a select group of textile and apparel companies, insisting that carpets or garments using the new fiber meet Monsanto's rigid quality standards. In return, Monsanto spends millions each year on pull-through promotion aimed at consumers. Without producing consumer goods, Monsanto's Chemstrand division finances consumer advertising to strengthen its synthetics market and to hold its distributors. Yet in other cases

---

18. Research Institute Staff, *Special Automation Report,* The Research Institute of America (December 31, 1964), p. 2.
19. Hubert Kay, "The Third Force in Urban Renewal," *Fortune,* Vol. LXX, No. 4 (October, 1964), p. 214.

center ownership of distribution facilities proves prudent. [JOHN L. GILLIS, Marketing Vice-President, Monsanto, discussing the establishment of 200 Monsanto Agricultural Centers, outlets for agricultural chemicals — *It was a matter of deciding whether to go into competition with our customers, the dealers. We decided they weren't doing the kind of job we could do ourselves, so we moved in.*] [20] In an affluent society with created wants, the largest profit hopes tend to be in marketing-oriented activities where the firm can wield some control over its own demand.

Periphery enterprises are sometimes moved into the center to preserve an *assured source of supply*. We have already mentioned the encroachment of mass retailers into manufacturing as typified by Sears. Not all backward integrating retailers are as large and socially visible. The Zale Corporation, with 411 jewelry stores, first approached ailing Elgin, its largest watch supplier, with the cosigning of a large loan. Zale now names six members of Elgin's nine-man board of directors. [MORRIS B. ZALE, President, Zale Corporation — *When Elgin got into this shape, we couldn't see them go broke. It wouldn't be good for us.*] [21]

Finally, pure conglomerates are absorbing healthy periphery firms as their entry ticket into the center. Growth into the center economy rarely comes to individual periphery firms, but clusters of former periphery enterprises directed by creative management can form a flying wedge and by avoiding industries already in the center can force their way to the top in little more than a decade. [RUPERT C. THOMPSON, Chairman, Textron — *Why fight GE or GM? We'd rather be a major factor in small industries, where the growth potential is generally better. We prefer those industries where the price of entry is high and where considerable technical skill is required.*] [22]

For a variety of reasons, then, the periphery is a happy hunting ground for center invaders and for pure conglomerates aspiring toward center membership. The periphery economy's continued existence is heavily conditioned by center economy strategy. Technical changes emanating from the center can force a restructuring of periphery organization. Center firm

20. *Forbes*, Vol. 96, No. 2 (July 15, 1965), p. 21.
21. *Forbes*, Vol. 96, No. 6 (September 15, 1965), p. 26.
22. *Forbes*, Vol. 96, No. 11 (December 1, 1965), p. 35.

distribution or factor-supply bottlenecks often induce direct center intervention in former periphery domains. And ambitious but unorthodox entrepreneurs buy their way into center status by spreading center techniques and organizational economies into periphery industries hitherto overlooked by diversifying giants.

The individual periphery firm is economically weak because it is economically small. The center economy is defined by unlimited potential, and potential is directly related to economic size. The most important long-run attributes of any firm are the *availability of funds* (internal and external) and the *quality of its management*. Given adequate funds and creative management, center firms can diversify, decentralize, integrate vertically and horizontally (when antitrust will allow), and embrace new technologies. Inherent financial limitations and inappropriate managerial structures effectively prohibit periphery firms from utilizing these essentials of long-run survival and prosperity.

One major point to be reiterated often: economic size yields the potential for acquiring adequate funds and creative management, but it is the actual acquisition of these twin assets and their use which erodes the periphery firm environment. To the extent that center firms act like periphery firms, denying their center potential, they allow a thriving periphery appendage. [PROFESSOR JOEL DIRLAM — *The absence of diversification of large steel firms is, perhaps, surprising. Large firms in steel have been unwilling or unable to diversify out of steel, in spite of their sizable internal flow of funds and in spite of the fact that the industry is characterized by excess and obsolescent capacity and by steadily increasing competition by substitutes. A partial explanation may be that steel executives regard themselves not as having gone into a business but having adopted a way of life, which was also characteristic of railroad executives until the new generation typified by Ben Heineman of Chicago and North Western.*][23]

Absolute size, not relative market strength, defines center membership. Even though it has a precarious foothold in auto-

23. U.S. Senate, Committee on the Judiciary, *Economic Concentration: Mergers and Other Factors Affecting Industry Concentration*, Part II, U.S. Government Printing Office, 1965, p. 767.

mobiles, its principal market, American Motors is a center firm. Yearly sales in the $1 billion dollar class assure them an adequate cash flow, but cash flow alone cannot do more than reinforce managerial talent. Should American Motors or any other center firm refuse to use its survival potential, should it persist in acting like a periphery firm, it stands vulnerably exposed to the periodic possibility of a fatal accident so common in periphery circles. Perhaps the directors of pure conglomerates, presently building new center participants from the raw materials of scientific potential and managerial talent, are uniquely situated for appraising the center firm's true long-run strength. [ROY L. ASH, President, Litton Industries — *We're not limited by our markets—the opportunities there are limitless. And we're not limited by our financial resources—we have $40 million in cash, another $70 million in bank credit available. Therefore we say: Our growth is determined and limited only by the ability of management. We say: If we fail to maintain our growth, management alone will be responsible.*][24]

The periphery economy is shaped by and limited to an industrial environment largely outside its sphere of influence. That periphery firms have short-run horizons and attitudes is not surprising. Why look to a future one cannot determine? If members of the loyal opposition, periphery firms are dependent on center pricing protection and market inaction. If free agents, they are limited to economic areas that the center does not effectively touch—a narrowing crack in the dynamic American economy.

Satellitic periphery firms are forced into simulated perfect competition by their center dependency. Backward satellites, selling their output to center firms, are classic pricetakers; center buyers capable of producing their own raw materials inputs pay backward satellites but little more than an estimated center firm production cost. They, therefore, present their smaller suppliers with horizontal demand curves not far above the minimum cost of periphery production. Center buyers may, however, be unwilling to purchase all that the periphery firm chooses to produce at this price. Perfect competition, the analytical crux of

24. *Forbes,* Vol. 93, No. 7 (April 1, 1964), p. 14.

neoclassical economics, is not dead in the American economy. It exists in almost pure form wherever satellites sell to center firms, for a *phantom competition* of threatening center firm backward integration promotes a highly competitive center entry price above which the market price cannot rise. No matter how few in number backward satellites may be, the phantom production of center firms keeps them virtually purely competitive.

Forward satellites are maintained only so long as they provide satisfactory efficiency and volume. When sales volume is closely related to price, as it commonly is except during the peak of prosperity, forward satellite prices are also closely circumscribed by center firm objectives. Here again, the phantom competition of direct entry potential forces competitive pricing.

The Prospects for Periphery Survival

THE periphery economy has played an important role in the American economy since its colonial beginnings. We should maintain a healthy skepticism about its imminent collapse. The first half of the 1960's were a period of rising prosperity, when accumulating center firm liquidity encouraged expansion by merger. Yet there are long-run indications that the periphery's recent trials are becoming permanent. Evidences that technological change is moving at an accelerated pace are omnipresent, and a dynamic technology is always a menace to traditional periphery management. And a high level of Federal research funds, the financial prime mover incipient in recent innovations, seems permanent.

International trade, a center firm specialty, will likely quicken, particularly for new products and processes developed in the advanced countries. Pure conglomerates, and older center firms seeking diversification, are now more actively raiding the periphery than ever before. They are, no doubt, spurred to do so by prosperity, but there are indications that the U.S. government is learning to use fiscal and monetary tools to avoid future recessions. The 1964 federal tax cut was the first ever enacted to forestall an impending economic decline. Is perpetual prosperity genuinely in the offing? If so, when will aggressive center firms lose their vigor?

The American consumer may lose little and gain much from center economy spread. Even the fortunate and resourceful periphery entrepreneur who finds financial solace within a conglomerate structure or through the use of center management brokers will prosper. Is it the microeconomic theorist who stands to lose the most as the periphery economy recedes, diminishing the economic reality that his intricately woven and carefully refined analytical tools are designed to describe? He, too, must now turn his attention to the ever-expanding center where periphery theory is of little use.

6. The Economics of the Center Firm

THE CENTER FIRMS' DISTINCTIVENESS stems from size and independence—from their owners, industry, product mix, and national origin; and secondly, from their intense awareness of the total economy, their long-run destiny, and the nature and drift of technical change. The center economy contains firms combining an economic "subjectivity," a consciousness of their active place in the total economic arena (an attitude shared with most periphery firms), with an "objectivity," the ability to observe the total economy's impact on the firm. The center's long-run power to influence the direction of technology and the organization of production creates a new territory for theoretical exploration. The well-worn map provided by conventional microeconomics is of limited use on the business frontiers of the center economy.

A Definition of the Center Firm

CENTER FIRMS, through structural metamorphosis, have freed themselves from the conventional restraints on firm growth. *The center economy is composed of those firms whose long-run average cost curves potentially rise as capacity increases, but may not actually do so.* Center firms have thwarted *potential* increases in their long-run costs in several ways. They have circumvented the diseconomies of greater-than-optimum plant size by duplicating plant facilities; a single product can be produced in many plants as firm output increases, with every plant approaching the size of operations giving optimum efficiency. Such sister plants are quite common. In 1954 40 percent of the 38,000 largest manufacturing plants were operated by companies running other large plants making the same product.[1]

The cost of most raw material inputs can be minimized through quantity purchase savings, backward integration (including both ownership and satellite control), and threats of vertical integration. The price of capital tends to fall for developing center firms as their credit rating rises, their securities assume blue-chip status, and internal funds accumulate. Labor costs per unit can often be reduced through the substitution of capital for labor, a process made especially appealing by the significant technical breakthroughs in capital equipment design. M. A. Adelman found that employment among the top 200 firms was about 60 percent more capital intensive than in the economy as a whole.[2] Decentralization minimizes, if it does not prevent, rising managerial costs per unit associated with center firm expansion.

Freed from the inevitability of rising costs, the center firm, while encountering limits to its rate of advance, can escape a host of restraints on its ultimate size. Convention once presented the principle of diminishing returns to characterize normal limitations on all firms' size. The principle postulates that if one of the four factors of production—land, labor, capital, or management—is fixed (relative to the other factors), costs per unit will rise beyond some output range. Certainly as a mathematical and physical principle, diminishing returns is valid. It remains an effective force limiting the size of firms in the periphery. Managerial resources for diminishing-returns circumvention have not always existed and are even now unavailable to most small enterprises. But for center firms, diminishing returns simply pro-

1. U.S. Senate, Committee on the Judiciary, *Economic Concentration, Part I, Overall and Conglomerate Aspects,* U.S. Government Printing Office, 1964, p. 269.
2. M. A. Adelman, "The Measurement of Industrial Concentration," *Review of Economics and Statistics,* Vol. XXXIII (1951), p. 278.

vide a series of potential bottlenecks. Factor restraints can and do precipitate crises in firm growth, but the prime function of center management is to surmount such obstacles. Stated graphically, it is the responsibility of center management to transform U-shaped cost curves into L-shaped ones.

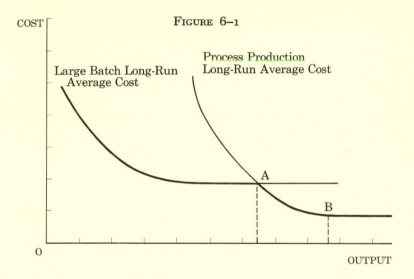

COST

FIGURE 6–1

Large Batch Long-Run Average Cost

Process Production Long-Run Average Cost

A

B

O

OUTPUT

Figure 6-1 shows two L-shaped long-run average cost curves. One depicts the firm's average long-run costs as output increases using a large batch technique, while the other shows average costs to the same firm (but a different plant) using process or continuous flow techniques. At low levels of output process production is not economically feasible, but beyond point A process production yields significant cost reductions. Beyond point B production costs become constant using the process method. L-shaped long-run curves assume that management inefficiency does not offset economies of scale accruing to other factors as output expands through time.

As the center firm grows it undoubtedly encounters both economies and diseconomies of scale. For long-run average costs to rise, the diseconomies must eventually overcome the admitted scale economies. Most discussions of the diseconomies of scale emphasize management's weighty bureaucracy, the red-tape labyrinth and communications difficulties found in any large organization. Beyond some size, so the theory instructs, management becomes highly inefficient and the main function of coordination collapses. In the periphery economy such is certainly the case. For example, those periphery firms operated by one tough-minded, inner-directed man cannot function under his personal direction if they get too large. The tycoon, no matter how shrewd and competent, is finally buried under an avalanche of details. Should he perform, for a time, a superhuman management task, it is unlikely that a man of his skill will grace the firm's on-coming generation.

In contrast, the greatest strength of center firms comes from their independence of one man. Important decisions are made by committees, so that a single individual's lack of vision is counterbalanced. What is lost by the large corporation failing to attract or to hold the brilliant, headstrong individualist entrepreneur—the one who envisions, designs, and establishes a new company or product—is often regained by the center firm buying the new enterprise, freeing the entrepreneur to push on toward new frontiers. To avoid a corporate cult of personality, the presidency of center firms is a post commonly awarded to a man within hailing distance of retirement. Authority and power do not simply flow down from the top, as organization charts suggest; they are divided and subdivided into manageable proportions.

In a center firm, dispersion of short-run decisions means that the efficiency of management is as high as the quality and training of the men on the management team. From all indications the quality of center management is superior. The center firm can offer greater promotion opportunities than its periphery rivals; it contains a greater variety of career patterns. With its high prestige, the center firm can recruit managerial talent directly from leading colleges and universities. Decentralization allows the large firm to offer as much responsibility as the periphery firm, while the excellent center firm training programs provide the needed expertise.

What has developed from its early beginning with the Pennsylvania Railroad is a new factor of production—staff management, the guardian of the long run. Once the early pattern of staff-and-line organization was incipient, American center firms continued to embrace and adapt a technology of management fashioned to free the firm from increasing managerial costs per unit. There is considerable evidence suggesting that managerial unit costs remain constant or perhaps decrease even when the largest firms expand.[3] It is even possible that the present pattern of extreme decentralization is but a transitional phase necessitated by a level of managerial technology now being superceded. Under way is a movement back to a limited centralization in some of the largest firms.[4]

Center Firm Growth

IF MANAGERIAL and other potential diseconomies of scale are not brakes on center firm growth and efficiency but merely resistances to be overcome by men skilled in the art of long-run cost curve deflation, no *economic* forces exist to prevent a single well-managed center firm from monopolizing most industrial markets. There are, of course, legal barriers in the form of antitrust laws, but if center firms have achieved constant long-run average cost curves, there is nothing, save the power of government and public opinion, to prevent the firm with the *lowest* costs from assuming the full burden of production for a specific product. So long as potential entry remained open to other firms, prices in such markets would probably reflect costs reasonably well.

Fear of antitrust prosecution does limit a single firm's participation in particular markets, but the antitrust division has not, except in rare instances, been effective in preventing center firm expansion by diversification. As a rule, center firms may not take more than a given percentage of a particular market, but they may participate in noncompeting markets. Thus diversifica-

3. Much of the evidence is summarized in William T. Morris, *Management Science in Action*, Richard D. Irwin, Inc., 1963, pp. 45–49; see also Michael Gort, *Diversification and Integration in American Industry*, Princeton University Press, 1962, p. 7.
4. Gilbert Burck, "Management Will Never Be the Same Again," *Fortune* (August, 1964).

tion frees center firms from the limits imposed by the size of any particular market, just as advances in the science of management release them from the bondage of rising long-run costs.

In theory-of-the-firm language, profitable multiproduct-firm expansion can proceed when the firm's marginal cost (the average of product marginal costs) is below the firm's marginal revenue (the average of product marginal revenues). We defined center firms as those whose expansion does not necessarily precipitate rising long-run average costs. Yet even if the firm's marginal cost falls as output increases, a firm's marginal revenue falling at a rapid rate will eventually overtake the gently declining cost curve, circumscribing continued growth. Here dynamic diversification provides the liberating force. Plant-loading diversification helps carry overhead costs, but more important the addition of new products with higher marginal revenue potential than the firm's average, accompanied by the periodic deletion of commodities with marginal revenue well below the firm's average, keeps the vigilant center firm's "average" marginal revenue curve bouyant.

When aggregate demand is rising in the economy, transforming "luxury" goods into social "necessities," and when technology is providing new products, a pool of high marginal revenue items is available. In a growing, progressive economy, center firms can keep their growth path unencumbered by remaining constantly alert to potential high marginal revenue additions to the firm's catalogue, while discarding the lowest marginal revenue commodities when they prove an intolerable drag on the firm's marginal revenue, without offering offsetting reductions in overhead. The falling revenue pinch is confined to specific products; product-mobile center firms can escape its bite when a prosperous economy generates fertile marginal revenue fields. [CRAWFORD H. GREENWALT, President, DuPont — . . . *you might liken a healthy business to a barrel that is set to catch rain water. When it rains new developments, the level of the barrel increases. On the other hand, you have to have a drain at the bottom to take out those things that have become marginal and constitute a drain on the resources of your management. Only if you have that drain at the bottom will the contents of your barrel remain fresh and healthy. The freshness of the contents of the barrel is really what counts for us. The size of the barrel will take care of itself.*] [5]

The new mode of center firm operations suggests an answer to the question posed by Professor R. H. Coase in 1937, "Why is not all production carried on by one big firm?" [6] For center firms, the primary external restraints are at present noneconomic. (1) Other firms, often large ones, occupy the firm's traditional markets where its efficiency is greatest. Such competitors will not merge, and in any event would not be permitted to merge by the Federal government. (2) As a center firm expands, all of its new activities come under closer government scrutiny. Antitrust funds are indeed limited, so antitrusters more often than not focus their attacks on the prominent center firms. (3) Center firms often grow by rationalizing sectors of the economy that have hitherto been small scale, poorly coordinated; if center firms expand in a stagnant economy, such opportunities may become more limited as a stable environment becomes less susceptible to rationalization.

In a rapidly growing economy, the third restraint on center firms will not be effective. Internal restraints, primarily capital and management deficiencies, provide the most important limits to the *rate* of center firm expansion in a growing economy, although they are unlikely to ever halt center firm growth. Center enterprises can obtain considerable capital on favorable terms from both internal and external sources, but they cannot obtain unlimited capital from either source. Retained earnings and depreciation allowances cannot be accumulated above some maximum rate and, furthermore, bankers are unwilling to commit funds without limit to any particular firm. Thus center firm capital must be allocated to its most efficient use; that is, it must be used to break the most threatening factor bottlenecks. Used to increase managerial salaries or to purchase factor suppliers or product retailers or to substitute machinery for labor, flexible

5. Quoted in C. Addison Hickman, "The Entrepreneural Function: The South as a Case Study," in Melvin Greenhut and W. Tate Whitman, *Essays in Southern Economic Development,* University of North Carolina Press, 1964, pp. 79–80.

6. R. H. Coase, "The Nature of the Firm," *Economica,* New Series, Vol. IV (1937), p. 394. Reprinted in Kenneth Boulding and George Stigler (eds.), *Readings in Price Theory,* Richard D. Irwin, Inc., 1952, pp. 331–351.

capital allocation is a potent cost reducing weapon. But it cannot in a limited period of time do unlimited duty.

Capital unavailability may partially retard the rate of center firm growth even in prosperous times, but the most important internal inhibitor of center firm growth in a growing economy is the managerial one. Management restraints include: (1) entrepreneural conservatism—many center firms show a pronounced aversion to multiple new investments, limiting their growth to those areas promising reliable returns; (2) susceptibility to organizational stress—every organization tends to slacken unless under stress, but too rapid growth turns stress into frustration; the stress factor sets an optimal rate of growth beyond which efficiency falls; (3) personnel limitations—as the firm expands, new managerial recruits must be assimilated into the firm's corporate style—a time-consuming process. Even when the firm grows by merger, retaining the old management, assimilation must still take place. Assimilated management is perhaps the greatest hindrance to rapid center firm growth, providing one explanation for large executive salaries at the center.

So long as the total economy grows satisfactorily, center firms face only restraints on their *rate* of growth, not barriers to prevent them from expanding. The impetus for growth springs from several sources. Small firms seek growth to take advantage of the familiar economies of scale: specialization of labor, installation of large units of equipment capable of producing lower unit costs if fully employed, economies of mass buying. But the quest for such economies becomes self-perpetuating. Firm growth permits the flourishing nonproduction work force to be divided into engineers, salesmen, financial specialists, research workers, but the division of labor creates perpetual imbalances. As the firm expands, it adds a new specialized department; if the new specialty is totally exploited, the firm must reach a certain size. In so doing other departments are added, requiring still further growth. The process of balance can be never ending, creating a perpetual impetus to growth.[7]

Personal reasons are also important. The majority of top corpo-

7. Edith Penrose, *The Theory of the Growth of the Firm*, Basil Blackwell & Mott, Ltd., 1959, pp. 68–71.

rate managers spend most of their professional life with a single firm. Ambitious men who identify with the firm's success, they know, as they approach the top of the managerial pyramid, that their chances of further promotion are enhanced by the firm's growth. Since most new positions are filled internally, the manager who fosters growth by creating a new division or department recommends himself for the top position in the new structure. In addition, the corporate salary pyramid corresponds rather closely to the organizational pyramid, with salaries at the top being elevated by additions to the firm's organizational base. Then, too, in business as elsewhere, growth is a symbol of American success. The most able managers find the challenge of growth its own reward as it gives them a good opportunity to demonstrate their ability to the stockholders, to their superiors, and to themselves. Past successes are immediately capitalized, prompting stockholders to demand continuing successful decisions. Management is interested in security as well as growth, but these two goals are complementary ones in a dynamic economy as long as the rate of firm expansion remains near the optimal rate.[8]

Center firms dwell in many markets; their top managerial eye is fixed on the long run. It is perfectly true that in the short run there is some increase in output that will radically increase center firm unit costs. Even when center firms hold excess industry capacity, these unused facilities are often technologically inferior. Their use may increase costs appreciably. Nonetheless center firms are not primarily concerned with short-run problems, for they have long since passed the dangers of infant mortality where the short run may be the only run. Center firms believe that they have achieved eternal life, and they act accordingly. First, their planning is more concerned with secular *shifts* in demand curves than with their elasticity. Second, they do not maximize short-run profit by restricting output and raising price as oligopoly theory predicts, for to do so would invite poor public relations and endanger long-run survival. Rather there is evidence that many center firms seek to maximize sales revenue subject to

---

8. For an interesting discussion of managerial motives and corporate growth, see Robin Marris, *The Economic Theory of "Managerial" Capitalism*, The Free Press of Glencoe, 1964, Chapter 2.

a profit restraint as Professor Baumol suggests.[9] And last, center firms are as concerned with long-run favorable government policy as with short-run windfall gains from government action.

Center firm operations reverse many platitudes. Among men, the old must face squarely man's mortality, their own lives having become short run. But not so for firms. The young and the small must face the perilous first few years when business death rates are astronomical. Successful middle-aged firms may harbor strong memories of their period of short-run struggles, but the comparatively old, better-established firms in the center economy have outlived and outgrown the traumas of year-to-year existence. Center firms have reached an age and a position enabling them to become the statesmen of business. They can set aside petty bickerings, for in the long run they share the total economy's fate.

Economic Implications of the Center Firm

ONCE THE center economy and the principles of its operation are examined, we are led to startling conclusions. The Soviet economy is often presented as a rough analogue to the U.S. economy were the latter operated by a single giant corporation. Given the internal structure of center firms, the purely *economic* forces that prevent just this from happening to most of the manufacturing and distributing sectors in the very long run are few indeed. There are, to be sure, certain activities in this area unsuited to large firms. Methods requiring quick adaptation to changing conditions, close personal supervision of details, and the benefits of the very small plant yield grudgingly, if at all, to large-scale performance. Even the Soviet Union retains a small private non-agricultural sector. And the upper limits imposed by optimal center firm growth rates assure that the process would take a very long time even if gained through multiple center firm mergers. But there seems no reason to believe that America's managerial elite, if merged under a single corporate dome, could not in time

9. William J. Baumol, *Business Behavior, Value and Growth,* The Macmillan Company, 1959, Chapters i and vi. The Baumol hypothesis receives tentative confirmation in Joseph W. McGuire, John S. Y. Chiu, and Alvar O. Elbing, "Executive Incomes, Sales and Profits," *American Economic Review,* Vol. LII (1962).

effectively allocate resources for virtually the entire manufacturing-distributing economy.

In 1890, when Marshall's brilliant synthesis of microtheory
appeared, the center economy was just beginning to form. Ironi-
cally, after the passage of the Sherman Act in that same year,
it seemed likely that at least in this country the center would be
nipped in the bud. So the theory, when conceived, adequately
described almost all firms not supported by monopoly; these
firms Marshall dealt with separately. Only in recent years has it
become evident that the U.S. government will not in the foreseeable future break up most firms in the center to make them conform to the perfectly competitive model. While economists still
hotly debate the merits of the theory, the center economy seems
fated beyond its constructs.

Economists are neither so foolish nor so tradition bound that
they cling to an obsolete theory enervating their analysis. Quite
the contrary. Many of the economic problems that have provided
the primary theoretical concerns for economic practitioners yield
satisfactorily to an analysis assuming that the total economy is
composed of periphery firms. This is true because the center
economy is, in the short run, a stabilizing element in most non-
technological respects. The vast majority of economic theory,
both micro and macro, is inherently short run. As the father of
macroeconomics once blandly put it, in the long run we are all
dead. But as human life expectancy increases and economic time
contracts, we are beginning to move into the economic long, long
run where problems of secular change become pressing.

Nevertheless in a considerable number of short-run problem
areas where economists have achieved notable success, the assumption of a totally periphery economy remains useful. In the
field of business cycles, for example, it is clear that *the periphery
economy is a prime disrupter of prosperity.* For the postwar period, there is strong evidence that profit margins on sales of
smaller manufacturing corporations lead the business cycle, turning down before the profit margins at the cycle peak for all manufacturing corporations. The average lead of profit margins at the
cycle peak for manufacturing corporations *below* $100 million of
assets is a year and a quarter, while the lead for manufacturing

corporations *over* the $100 million mark is only two-quarters of a year. (Comparable noncorporate figures are not available, but would surely reinforce the same tendency.) Professor Howard J. Sherman summarizes the evidence in this way:

> The smaller and more competitive firms are the first to be affected by the profit squeeze in prosperity because of the increasing numbers of inefficient firms in their ranks, because of their greater sensitivity to credit restriction, and because of their lesser ability to maintain prices. The fact of their earlier decline in profit margins strongly implies that *it is these smaller firms that precipitate the depression,* since the decline in their profit margins is soon followed by a decline in their investment decisions and expenditures. The fact that the large oligopolistic firms often maintain their own investment expenditures for some time after the cycle turning point is not sufficient to stop the depression that is already under way and spreading to all areas of industry.[10]

In assuming that the periphery economy is the total economy, business-cycle theorists ignore the most important sources of production and investment. But their unrealistic assumptions do fit the most volatile source of investment expenditure. For the analysis of short-run fluctuations it is enough to understand the catalytic element. In terms of short-run shifts in investment, the periphery economy leads the downturn, pulling aggregate economic activity and eventually center firm activity into a recession unless government provides a countervailing economic force.

Periphery firms, though less critical than center firms in total manufacturing output, are often during prosperity prime movers of the short run. The currently available short-run, periphery economy theory provides a powerful tool for handling such important matters. It is secular, long-run theory that has fallen into intellectual poverty since the writings of the classical economists and Marx. In the long run, shifts in demand and changes in

10. Howard J. Sherman, *Introduction to the Economics of Growth, Unemployment and Inflation,* Appleton-Century-Crofts, 1964, p. 158.

technology provide pivotal disruptions—of the two, technological changes are probably more important.[11] And the most important technology shapes, and is shaped by, firms in the center economy.

A stabilizing influence in the short run, center firms maintain their considerable investment expenditures in the face of falling short-term profit expectations as long as long-run prospects appear favorable. Yet it is center firms which often provide the primary means of secular disruption through the large-scale, if sometimes belated, introduction of new products and new technology. Center firms do not provide the greater part of invention —large, bureaucratic organizations are poorly suited for most individualistic, creative activity. What they do provide is the organizational means for turning inventions into marketable innovations; they excell in rapidly transforming profitable new ideas and products into established commodities. If roving center firms are numerous enough to assume new entry into technically retarded markets with new innovations, and so long as foreign competitors are allowed reasonable access to U.S. markets, competition in terms of product innovation, coupled with the remaining elements of traditional price competition, seems likely to provide restraints as powerful as those furnished by intense short-run price competition in the periphery economy. Loyal opposition periphery competitors, in the industries where there are many effective ones, can be depended on to drive established commodity prices downward when they begin to feel the impact of declining demand. Thus center firms cannot, with rare exceptions, depend on high profit margins unless fresh areas are sighted. While the loyal opposition applies pressure within the industry, other center firms offer potential industry entry. With reasonable interindustry stability, the metals enterprises in the center, for example, now face both foreign invasion and entry into many

11. The importance of technological progress for American economic growth is stressed in Robert M. Solow, "Technical Change and the Aggregate Production Function," *Review of Economics and Statistics,* Vol. XXXIX (1957); also B. F. Massell, "Capital Formation and Technological Change in United States Manufacturing," *Review of Economics and Statistics,* Vol. XLII (1960). John W. Kendrick, *Productivity Trends in the United States,* Princeton University Press, 1961, is also useful. Technical progress is commonly embodied in new capital equipment, making the separation of capital accumulation from technical progress very difficult.

of their markets by chemical center firms, while petroleum center firms migrate into numerous chemical markets.

The Center Firm and the Short Run

FOR THE LONG RUN, center firm activity is pivotal. Yet like periphery firms, actions of center economy residents have short-run repercussions. We must balance our examination of the center economy by considering its impact on a central microeconomic goal—the efficient allocation of resources. Under capitalism, the supreme goal of resource allocation is the maximization of total consumer satisfaction. Since, it is granted, no one can better maximize an individual's consuming satisfaction than the individual himself, he must, for those goods and services susceptible to private sector distribution, be given a free hand in the allocation process. Consumers must be allowed to determine what is produced and in what quantity. They can make their decisions effective only if prices, the primary allocative mechanism in a market economy, are reasonably responsive to changes in consumer taste and income. How has the spread of large, multiproduct firms affected consumer control of production?

The theory of the firm tells us that, under perfect competition, consumers have virtually complete control over price (assuming costs constant). No perfectly competitive firm has any control over price. As we move away from perfect competition through monopolistic competition, oligopoly, and monopoly, individual firms achieve increasing control over the pricing mechanism, and hence over allocation. Assuming, as the theory does, that firms maximize short-run profits, it can easily be shown that a higher price and a smaller output will occur as enterprises gain increasing price authority. Thus perfect competition best facilitates consumer satisfaction, leaving *as it does* the critical price mechanism in the possession of those who best know how to maximize their own consumption welfare.

Such a theory encounters at least three fundamental objections. It assumes that the structure of wants is known by consumers and that they are formulated free of firm influence. The pervasive power of advertising is ignored. Research is also overlooked. Under perfect competition, the firm's equilibrium profits are so limited that they cannot finance product improvement and development, yet such expenditures may substantially improve the welfare of consumers. Last, the theory assumes that firms maximize short-run profits by producing at the level of output where the cost of the last unit produced equals its price. If firms do not maximize short-run profits, if they do not know what their marginal costs are, the system may not yield the expected results.

Center firms violate the system in the three ways mentioned above: they use advertising to influence the pattern of consumer wants; they change the form and substance of consumable items through research; and, if Professor Baumol is correct, they refuse to maximize short-run profits. Also, when the center economy spreads, a growing number of important transactions become interfirm transactions. When center firms integrate vertically, they internalize external economies of scale. Interfirm allocation resembles market allocation only when interfirm prices resemble market prices. Transfer prices within the firm may not equal market prices because (1) there are no sales taxes on nonmarket transactions, and (2) interfirm prices may be discounted, reflecting the advantages accruing to the firm from trading with itself rather than with outsiders.

Internal price distortions are not, however, likely to be very serious. Facing a more serious problem from this source, the Soviets attempt to rationalize internal prices by using international prices as a guide; for the Soviet Union the cost of marginal inputs is the international price. U.S. center firms are more fortunate; they can use the less distorted domestic price structures of companion enterprises in the U.S. economy for guidance. More importantly, center firms do not operate at outputs that equate marginal costs with marginal revenues; they do not maximize short-run profits. Diversified center firms cannot know even the average cost of producing a particular product with accuracy. For the multiproduct firm, a large portion of costs are joint costs. In addition to the well-known economies of large-scale research, significant center firm economies of scale include: (1) increased advertising effectiveness per dollar spent, precipitated by quantity discounts from the mass media; (2) reduced capital costs—depreciation allowances and retained earnings carry no direct interest charges; they are free funds in the real sense, although not in the opportunity cost sense;   (3) quantity buying and the by-passing of intermediaries;   (4) more effective utilization of personnel; most white-collar workers, and increasingly, blue-collar ones as well, represent fixed costs that can be reduced per unit by intensive specialization. How can the contribution of a particular product to such scale economies be evaluated?

There is no way to impute joint costs to specific products using the production function of a multiproduct firm.[12] Multiproduct firms can meaningfully compute marginal joint costs for the firm, but not for any single product. When some portion of joint cost is arbitrarily assigned to specific products, and such assignment cannot but be arbitrary, price and output decisions based on these costs contain an element of irrationality. Thus multiproduct firms know something of the same irrational price problem that plagues Soviet planners. As Soviet planners use international prices as a guide, so multiproduct firms can use competitors' prices, but this in no way makes a path to rational pricing. Competitors will either be multiproduct firms, and hence in the same boat, or single-product firms with totally different, probably higher, cost curves.

Furthermore, center firms are probably more interested in stabilizing profits than in maximizing them. Where ownership is divorced from control, that part of profits distributed to stockholders becomes a cost to management, and stable costs make easier planning. Profit stability reduces the excessive expectations from unions and stockholders that may accompany a few years of unusually high earnings.

Finally, the expansion of the diversified center economy into a new industry tends to retard the mobility of resources, enervating the response to changing consumer demands. Center firms may retain a line of products which their accounting system dubs unprofitable to keep the personnel hierarchy intact, especially the management personnel if there is an impending possibility of shifting them to new areas in the future. When the deficit division

12. Peter J. D. Wiles, *Price, Cost, and Output* (Revised Edition), Frederick A. Praeger, Inc., 1963, pp. 110–111.

provides an outlet for the products of profitable divisions, it may pay to keep the lagging component in operation. The same is true if the unprofitable division is a major supplier to a profitable corporate component. Further, one or two low-profit operations may be useful to lower the firm profits in boom years, reducing union and stockholder demands.

By taking substantial control of the price mechanism from consumers, by refusing to maximize short-run profits, and by retarding the movement of resources, center firms inhibit consumer allocation of resources. In partial compensation, however, they increase the efficiency of satellite firms. Referring to backward satellites, Professor Adelman reports that:

> The dominant buyer makes his suppliers' demand curve highly elastic; if he can, he will equate the seller's price to marginal cost, thus satisfying Lerner's criterion that the market is partly competitive. But he will also attempt to make it perfectly competitive by increasing the knowledge of the participants, strengthening their foresight as to what may happen if they do not behave, and providing actual or potential entry into the industry.[13]

Satellitic periphery firms are forced by the center to realize the efficiency provided by near-perfect competition. They can then be saved from the concomitant financial and technical impoverishment inherent in a perfectly competitive existence by aid from the oligopolistic center. Sears, for example, gives such aid to its manufacturing suppliers from time to time. The growth in demand for the products of backward satellites is tied to the growth for the center's products, but periphery firms are not usually allowed to grow as rapidly as this derived demand would warrant. Center firms commonly spread their purchases among a larger number of satellites when their input requirements increase, restricting backward satellites' growth. Should their satellites grow, notwithstanding center purchasing diffusion, the center firm involved is inclined to integrate vertically to escape a situation of countervailing power.

13. M. A. Adelman, "The Large Firm and its Suppliers," *Review of Economics and Statistics*, Vol. XXXI (1949), p. 116.

The Center Firm and the Banking Industry

THE CENTER ECONOMY is serviced by its own financial community, a financial auxiliary to center activities. While confined to a small cadre of distinguished banks located in major financial districts, competition for the center economy's banking business is, nonetheless, national in scope.[RUDOLPH A. PETERSON, President, Bank of America — *There are two parts to this banking business. First, there's the purely local business. The guy in Houston takes his money bags and checks downtown and clears them with his local bank. This is and probably always will be geographically oriented. Then, there's the job of participating in the financial programs of large corporations and the compensatory relationships that go with it. We feel we can ignore geography. We're already doing so, moving into New York, Philadelphia and Chicago to work with corporations.*][14] No competition within the commercial banking system is more price oriented. Center firm loan requirements are so large that only a fraction of the American banking community can compete for their financial trade. By one estimate, only 100 U.S. banks actively compete to serve the center's financial needs.[15]

Like other center buyers, the treasurers of center firms, constituting the demand side of this exclusive financial market, are sophisticated shoppers and extremely price conscious. Bidding for a highly homogeneous product, they bargain shop, canvassing the sources of high finance for low rates. Representing firms with impeccable credit credentials, they stand assured of securing their desired funds from banks or other financial intermediaries. Center firms hold accounts in several large banks; shifts in competitive appeal among banks is revealed by shifts in relative center deposit importance. Account splitting reflects in part an inevitable response to geographic dispersion, but it also reinforces the common center firm strategy of using depositor relationships as a bargaining point for securing preferential treatment.

14. *Forbes,* Vol. 98, No. 6 (September 15, 1966), p. 40.
15. A concise statement on center firm relations with banks is Deane Carson and Paul H. Cootner, "The Structure of Competition on Commercial Banking in the United States," in Commission on Money and Credit, *Private Financial Institutions,* Prentice-Hall, Inc., 1963, pp. 92–93.

U.S. law restricts ownership ties between U.S. banks and industrial corporations, but the prohibition does not extend to corporate ownership of foreign banks. The Dow Banking Corporation in Zurich, Switzerland, is a wholly owned bank of the Dow Chemical Company. [HERBERT D. DOAN, President, Dow Chemical — *We are chemists, not bankers, but proper finance is so important to us that we have gone into the banking business. . . .*][16]

Dow hopes the bank will make a profit, but its primary purpose is to lend financial aid to Dow's European customers. Dow, like other center firms, views money as just another input. [JOHN VAN STIRUM, Assistant Treasurer, Dow Chemical — *Using chemical terminology, we visualize Dow Banking Corporation as a financial catalyst between Dow companies, our bankers, and our customers, producing an essential raw material in scarce supply—medium term money.*] [17]

Resembling other center economy satellites, center-serving banks are presented with a horizontal demand curve for funds. No bank competing for center firm patronage can long maintain a prime rate of interest above that generally offered. The price of loanable funds to center clients is highly uniform, although center firms may choose not to borrow as much as banks desire to lend at the going rate. The cost to banks of center loans would be difficult to compute, but the prime rate conventionally offered approximates the Treasury bill rate, the closest asset substitute for center firm paper. In short, the price of borrowed money is effectively minimized by center firms. Money from external sources can nowhere be obtained for less. The nation's major financial institutions have come to serve the center as satellites, threatened by center invasion when their prices or services are unsatisfactory —an ironic twist, considering widespread fears of a few decades ago that the captains of finance would one day be the unchallenged kings of industry.

The center economy is surrounded and served by a legion of firms, financial and nonfinancial, pressed into a simulated perfect competition. The center transmits its own urgency and efficiency

16. *Business Week*, No. 1909 (April 2, 1966), p. 84.
17. *Ibid.*, p. 91.

to these encircling enterprises, projecting its own dynamism far beyond its immediate boundaries. Such in large measure is the center economy's contribution to the achievement of America's microeconomic goals. It is a noteworthy contribution.

Oligopolistic center economy production may rival the efficiency of more competitive periphery economy market structures for still another reason. Competitive markets necessitate severality of control. It is perfectly true, as commonly argued, that natural resources must be exploited as a unit to minimize the proliferation of uneconomic investments and to maximize the conservation of irreplacable materials. But should this argument be confined to natural resources? Severality of control abates the realization of scale economies in all industries, particularly the intangible economies of increased advertising effectiveness, reduced capital costs, and personnel specialization that know no industry bounds. Extreme severality of control, when accompanied by very small enterprise units as in the machine tool industry, may also remove the technical scale economies accompanying a shift upward in the technical hierarchy toward continuous flow production techniques. Severality of ownership, characteristic of center firms, does no violence whatsoever to efficiency; only the dispersion of control removes scale economies beyond everyone's reach.[18]

The Center Firm and Microeconomic Goals

ON BALANCE, the center economy has a mixed record when judged by the traditional microeconomic standards of rational allocation and efficiency. The center economy probably exceeds the periphery sector in efficiency, particularly when center firm influence on satellites is taken into account. But the inescapable joint cost problem introduces irrationality into prices and hence into allocation.

How well does the center economy perform in the macroeconomic spheres of stabilization and growth? We have previously seen that because of their comparative freedom of short-run profit expectations and short-term credit, center firms provide a non-

18. Wiles, *op. cit.*, pp. 277-280.

governmental stabilizing force. We also noted the evidence suggesting that center managers, partially liberated from the immediate demands of owners, often maximize sales subject to a minimum profit restraint. They optimize, but do not maximize, the growth of the firm's output given their cost and revenue positions. The widely accepted concept of the accelerator implies that many firms expand their capacity when demand and sales rise, rather than simply raising prices as they might if they took profit maximization dogmatically. The separation of ownership and control may have saved us from the output restriction that oligopolistic profit maximization in the short run would decree. Center firms cannot ignore considerations of efficiency because of their profit restraint, but neither do they overlook new investment possibilities crucial to growth. Center managers desire growth because it enhances their income and prestige and the firm's long-run survival chances; yet they cannot escape efficiency.

Does the center economy, then, provide the best of all possible worlds for efficiency growth? Have we been laying the analytical groundwork for a new managerial creed, praising center firms for promoting growth without neglecting the virtues of efficiency? Center firms do provide the islands of planning that prevent the U.S. economy from being virtually planless in its manufacturing-distributing sectors. And at their best, center firm planning mechanisms deserve a place among the world's most efficient and flexible. They have the extra virtue of being widespread enough to prevent a national crisis when a single planning unit fails. The center economy furnishes a laissez-faire market for planning, where the best planning mechanisms and the best planners tend to force bad planning out. Yet center economy planning may prove to be only a transitional phase between the largely planless nineteenth century and the nationally planned twenty-first. It is conceivable that regional and national planning, through the use of perfect computation, might realize the virtues of perfect competition without suffering from its vices.[19]

Even if the center economy serves us well, two reservations are in order. First, the inefficiency of severality of control is ob-

19. Perfect computation as a substitute for perfect competition is discussed in Peter J. D. Wiles, *The Political Economy of Communism*, Basil Blackwell & Mott, Ltd., 1962, pp. 147–150, 193–205.

viated by consolidating considerable economic power in center firms. Ignoring political implications, it is clear that the *direction* of research, innovation, and advertising expenditure is designed to allocate resources toward industries under center firm control. While invading areas where demand is rising, center firms try with some effect to maintain or increment demand in areas they already occupy. One result is what Professor Galbraith calls social imbalance between the affluent private and starved public sectors.[20] But within the private sector, there exists a corresponding imbalance between the affluent center economy and the poverty-stricken periphery. We can only guess at the revolution that might be wrought in industries dominated by periphery firms if they received their proportionate share of finance and managerial talent.

Second, while diversified, decentralized oligopoly combines considerable efficiency with the transmutation of technological change, the center economy is not the most effective vehicle for generating new technology. The technology-creating function might better be performed by government-financed institutes of research, perhaps university affiliated, perhaps not. Government-financed agricultural research has fostered enormous productivity gains, exceeding those in the industrial sector during comparable periods. Center firms seem willing to follow the pull of technology, but they are probably not best suited for initiating that force promoting long-run organizational stress.

The Center Economy and Employment

THE RISE of the center economy in the late nineteenth and twentieth centuries has colored every aspect of economic activity. We have touched on the center's impact on allocation, efficiency, and growth. But what of the center economy's role in providing employment? During the postwar period investment has been both capital saving and labor saving,[21] necessitating an increasingly

---

20. John Kenneth Galbraith, *The Affluent Society,* Houghton Mifflin Company, 1958, Chapter XVIII.
21. Barring a fall in the interest rate, innovations must be labor saving. This point is forcefully made by Alvin H. Hansen, *The Postwar American Economy,* W. W. Norton & Company, Inc., 1964, p. 59. Bert G. Hickman, *Investment Demand and U.S. Economic Growth,* Brookings Institution, 1965, documents the capital-saving nature of postwar investment.

rapid rate of GNP growth to provide full employment. The spread of the center into new areas has helped furnish growth-inducing investment, but the long-run effects on the labor-output ratio are troublesome. The center tends to substitute capital for labor, and the encroachment of center firms into new markets erodes the employment potential of competing periphery enterprises. The total number of manufacturing firms was lower at the beginning of 1963 than in 1950.[22] Retail trade showed a gain in firms between 1951 and 1958, but this gain was the result of large increases in center satellites (principally motor vehicle dealers and gasoline stations) more than offsetting declines in the number of free agent general merchandise and food firms.[23] From 1951 to 1959, the number of firms in all industries rose by 12.8 percent. Only in manufacturing and retailing, the primary sectors of center influence, was the percentage rise less than average.[24] Between 1948 and 1961, the percentage of self-employed in wholesale and retail trade declined from 21.8 percent to 18.4 percent.[25]

Given a choice between efficiency and employment, most economists favor efficiency. Paul Samuelson undoubtedly voiced the prevailing professional opinion of the smaller periphery enterprises when he wrote:

> The only thing that can be said for such small businesses is that they make jobs. But the jobs they make are largely an illusion as far as pay is concerned, and represent boondoggling of as reprehensible and unnecessary a kind as would public-works projects aimed at simply digging holes and filling them in again.[26]

But are the people employed in small concerns likely to find a place in the efficient center economy? Very small businesses do employ some people with technical skill, business experience, or professional training who could find employment in center firms if the latter expanded sufficiently; but they also employ a large number of persons technically and personally outside the stan-

22. U.S. Department of Commerce, *Statistical Abstract of the United States,* Government Printing Office, 1964, Table 654, p. 487.

23. Betty C. Churchill, "Rise in the Business Population," *Survey of Current Business,* Vol. XXXIX (May, 1959), p. 16.

24. John H. Bunzel, *The American Small Businessman,* Alfred A. Knopf, Inc., 1962, p. 281.

25. John E. Bregger, "Self Employment in the United States, 1948–62," *Monthly Labor Review,* Vol. 86 (January, 1963), pp. 37–43.

26. Paul A. Samuelson, *Economics* (Fifth edition), McGraw-Hill, Inc., 1961, p. 553.

dards set by center concerns. These include the elderly,[27] those with physical handicaps, and men and women who are simply unable to function well in a complex, impersonal organization. Sociologists Seymour Lipset and Reinhard Bendix designate self-employment as "one of the few positions of higher status attainable by manual workers."[28] To deteriorate this means of social mobility for unskilled, semiskilled, and manual workers makes threadbare the lingering remnants of the American dream.

Many small-scale periphery firms belong in the residual employment category. They are the employers of last resort. Labor is a factor of production to be economized by management, but it is more than this. Labor is embodied in men, the means but yet the end of production. To complete our inspection of the two business economies, we must go to their respective work places.

27. Small firms are less reluctant to hire older workers for at least three reasons: (1) lack of seniority provisions requiring promotion from within, allowing older workers to be hired at other than lowest skill jobs; (2) fewer small firms have pension plans; (3) larger firms show stronger preference for younger workers. See R. C. Wilcock and W. H. Franke, *Unwanted Workers: Permanent Layoffs and Long-Term Unemployment*, Free Press of Glencoe, 1963, p. 147.

28. Seymour M. Lipset and Reinhard Bendix, *Social Mobility in Industrial Society*, University of California Press, 1959, p. 181.

7. The Labor Economics of Business Dualism

WHERE THERE IS INDUSTRY, there must be labor. And where there is industrial labor, we will likely find labor organizations. But labor unions represent only a fifth of the U.S. laboring population. Why is so much attention paid them by economists? The reasons are many. To name but one, unions provide an organized reflection of the economic forces affecting major industries. Even though trade unionism represents a numerical minority of the labor force, what happens within unions yields insights into the economic forces impinging on all American workers. No persistent ripple in the waters of economic structure leaves unions untouched. The history of labor's organized activities reproduces, with high fidelity, the worker's collective response to a multitude of social, political, and economic disturbances endemic to growing industrial economies. Although a distinct minority of American workers hold union cards, union membership is highly concentrated in important industrial sectors. Eighty percent of union membership is classified under manufacturing, construction, mining, and transportation-public utilities. Manufacturing, the industrial home of key industries, accounts for almost half of the total U.S. union membership strength. The importance of industrial unions, like that of center business firms, rests on industrial placement as well as labor force coverage.

Types of Labor Unions

LABOR ECONOMISTS have long recognized that unions are, for most purposes, best understood when divided into two or more classifications. The most common division sequesters craft unions from industrial unions. Strictly speaking, a craft union should include only workers in a particular type of skilled work, although most craft unions in the U.S. are amalgamated unions embracing several related trades. Narrowly defined, an industrial union should include only workers in a single industry. When choosing the broadest possible definition of "industry," one notices that the majority of large industrial unions still covers several industrial categories. The United Automobile Workers, for example, has large memberships in the Aircraft and Farm Machinery Industries. But in the common parlance, a craft union is composed of skilled workers in one or more closely related trades, while an industrial union organizes all workers in a plant regardless of their skill or function.

Another possible division of labor unions is by size. A few American unions are very large, many are minute. The six largest American unions are the Teamsters, the Automobile Workers, the Steelworkers, the Carpenters, the Electrical Workers (International Brotherhood of Electrical Workers), and the Machinists. Remembering that firm size was useful in differentiating the center from periphery firms, we may be tempted to apply the same criterion to define center and periphery labor. There are, indeed, correspondences between large unions, key industries, and center firms. The Teamsters are organized on a transportation base, the Carpenters in construction, but four of the largest six are rooted in various stages of our key manufacturing industries—sectors dominated, for the most part, by center firms. Clearly the large Auto Workers, Steelworkers, Electrical Workers, and Machinists do their most important bargaining with center firms. Just as clearly the very small Asbestos Workers; Bill Posters; Brick and Clay Workers; Cement, Lime and Gypsum Workers; Cigarmakers; Coopers; Doll and Toy Workers; and Glove Workers commonly pursue their organizational objectives in the periphery economy. Yet sheer size does not give unions the same potency, in terms of survival or specific goals, that it lends to business firms.

A third possible demarcation of union types is centralized unions versus decentralized ones. And here we strike a responsive note. Where the unionized firm sells in local markets, as in the building trades and service industries, the local union usually preserves its independence from the national office. Where the industry's product sells in national or international markets, the specifics of collective bargaining agreements are generally determined at the national level, leaving only the administrative task of supervising the predetermined settlement to the local union.[1] As we noted in Chapter 4, center firms are characterized by national markets and international markets while periphery enterprises operate more commonly in subnational markets.

Organized Labor and the Dual Economy

WHILE all of these distinctions, and many others, are essential to a thorough understanding of the economics of American labor, none forms a perfect correspondence with the division of business enterprise into center and periphery. Both center and periphery are organized by craft and industrial unions, since they employ skilled and unskilled labor. The center economy is the organizational home of large unions, but the enormous Teamsters and Carpenters unions have but slight center affiliation. Yet the extent to which union authority is concentrated at the top of the labor pyramid does relate unions to the center or periphery. Center firms sell their outputs in multiple markets, forcing unions to coordinate their bargaining efforts.

The demand for labor is a derived demand, dependent on the selling strength of the things labor produces. Thus it is not surprising that U.S. labor unions have, in part, a derived structure, an organizational configuration conditioned by the nature of the business firms with whom they negotiate. This is not to say that unions do not operate under their own peculiar organizational imperatives, for indeed they do. The structure of labor unions is

1. Albert Rees, *The Economics of Trade Unions*, University of Chicago Press, 1962, p. 26.

more than a mere reflection of the particular business environment they inhabit. But by combining the two sets of forces working to mold labor's organizational shape—the impact of business organization and industry characteristics *and* the special logic of unionism—we can best understand the relation of labor to business dualism and to the evolving future of the U.S. economy.

Given the dependence of several of the largest American unions on the center economy and their affinity with key industries, limited center business and large labor conformities are not unexpected. The characteristic center-firm administrative pattern, utilizing staff-and-line management, was pioneered by the railroads. Not surprisingly the railroad brotherhoods are among the oldest and most stable contemporary unions. New patterns in both labor and management were struck in America's first big business. Industrial unionism began when Eugene V. Debs formed the American Railway Union in 1893, a union open to all persons employed in railway service. Although the ARU suffered fatal defeat in the Pullman and Chicago strikes of 1894, the germ of industrial unionism was implanted in the same historic soil that nurtured the embryo of center business.

Most center firms, with the latter-day exception of center retailing, achieved prominence by riding the rise of economically strategic key industries to industrial maturity. Early union strength likewise emerged from a core of strategically placed workers in important industries—locomotive engineers in railroading, loom fixers in textiles, cutters in the garment industry, truckers in transportation. Thus strategic industrial placement was important in establishing both center firms and strong unions. Strong unions are even today confined in many industries to crafts playing a critical production role.

But the center economy and today's large unions share more than memories of a common history. In the center economy, where large plants abound, management must perform its decision making at a level remote from the experience and participation of workers. Just so, the large unions negotiating with center firms must bargain at some distance from the union local and the individual member. Like the center firm, large unions operate under an organizational imperative for *survival*. Since large unions represent members in many companies usually occupying more than one industry, survival demands that the union concern itself with issues involving the whole economy—for example, the adequacy of aggregate demand, the level of national employment, and human rights. To the extent that the center firm is diversified, it too must consider more than the needs of a single plant or division. Thus center firms and large unions tend to use a common vocabulary greater in scope than that used by the decentralized labor bargainers in, for example, construction.

The removal of collective bargaining to the national level and the accompanying subjugation of local issues bearing the most immediacy for the individual worker have alienated the rank and file worker from *both* the union and the firm. [UNITED AUTO WORKER *staff member #1* commenting on an opinion poll among aircraft workers taken by Lou Harris — *One of Harris' critical findings, I thought, was that workers felt that they were being encompassed by bigness within the unions as they have been by bigness within the corporations. . . . He got the idea that workers were alienated not only from the corporation but also from the union.*] [2] For the unions, still a political organization, this alienation at the grass roots is fundamental. Unlike the managers of center firms who have insulated themselves from the control of stockholders, the labor leadership must adhere to wishes of its members. Workers can do little about the depersonalized structure of the center corporation, but as union members they can act to oust the present leadership and, in most industrial states, vote on whether or not they want to be covered by the union shop.

Neither labor nor management is personally responsible for the removal of center-firm collective bargaining from the local level. Negotiations in the center economy have become quite complex, strengthening the role of legal and economic experts on the national union staff. Job evaluation, time-and-motion studies, pensions, medical benefits, and guaranteed annual wages are issues simply exceeding the training and capabilities of local union

2. Quoted from the Center for the Study of Democratic Institutions, *Labor Looks at Labor*, 1963, p. 6; a discussion of labor's contemporary problems by several anonymous trade union leaders from the United Auto Workers, identified only by number. The moderator was Paul Jacobs of the University of California, Berkeley.

officials. Intricate national labor legislation, direct Federal intervention in collective bargaining, and the rising incidence of arbitration also compound local union reliance on union staff lawyers and economists. Center firms have answered similar technical problems in other areas with decentralization, hiring well-qualified line managers to supervise corporate operations at the division or plant level. However, the imperatives of unionism have forced large unions to centralize their dealings with center firms, allowing initiative and enthusiasm to atrophy at the local level. [UAW *staff member #1 — The changing attitude of workers toward the trade union movement is really one of our major problems.*][3]

Exclusive attachment to traditional markets and structural inflexibility are the common enemies of institutional survival for both firms and unions. Certainly the business community yields prominent examples of managerial rigor mortis. And yet center firms have entered the turbulent sixties with uncommon organizational vigor. Even the long dormant railroads are beginning to move toward industrial diversity as salvation from their ruinous decline in demand. The Southern Pacific engages in equipment leasing; the Chicago and North Western has entered the chemical industry; the Kansas City Southern has a stake in a mutual investment fund; and the Bangor and Aroostook makes boats, jewelry, fabrics, and foundry equipment. The Pennsylvania Railroad owns a pipeline company in addition to land development companies with extensive holdings in Texas, Florida, and California. The railroad brotherhoods have shown no similar tendency to save their organizational lives by diversifying their jurisdictions.

While center firms got their initial growth through expanding sales in traditional markets, they have relied on vertical integration, geographical dispersion, and product diversification to sustain them when their mother industries faltered in growth prospects. Unions participating in the center economy have made some progress toward industrial diversification, but jurisdictional limitations imposed by brother unions sharply limit their center economy expansion. A few unions, notably the United Mine Workers Local 50 and the Teamsters, have tried to grow through

3. *Ibid.*, p. 5.

organizing the periphery economy, but their successes have been sporadic. As a result, the center economy's business firms spread their influence and increase their economic stature while their matched unions face membership declines except during periods of peak prosperity.

American unionism grew from a membership of 447,000 in 1897 to a high of 17,700,000 in 1957, declining by 1962 to 15,900,000. As a percent of the labor force, the union affiliation peak was 26 percent in 1953, declining to 21 percent by 1962. Over half the decline in union membership between 1953 and 1962 occurred in the ten largest unions, primarily among the center economy bargainers. The Auto Workers, the Steelworkers, and the Machinists sustained the heaviest membership losses.

The destiny of American labor has, from the beginning, been involved in the changing structures of the center and periphery economies. Before the center economy was formed in the nation's key industries, American business was very largely conducted in small, local firms. Consequently the American labor movement commenced as a nest of small, isolated unions with local interests. During most of America's economic history labor's primary strength resided not in strong national unions but among scattered locals attuned to their separate problems and destinies. A multitude of local unions retained their power and vitality while national unions, such as the Knights of Labor, flourished briefly, then perished abruptly. In labor as in business, strong local organizations preceded lasting national units. In 1886, just before the first wave of business mergers that permanently transformed the structure of American business, a number of national labor bodies came together to form the American Federation of Labor.

The early unions clustered around companies specializing in unit and small batch production—firms in the building trades, shoemaking, printing. Not until the great depression of the 1930's, when the Federal government forced the prostrate mass production industries to cease their militant and heretofore successful resistance toward unionization was labor successful in organizing steel and automobiles. Even with the government forcing mass production firms to acquiesce in organizing efforts, the craft-oriented AFL proved too inflexible in attitude and structure to organize masses of unskilled workers. A new type of national union, the Congress of Industrial Organizations (CIO), was formed to represent the largely unskilled mass production segment of the center economy.

Union Gains as a Collective Good

PRIOR TO the depression the overwhelming majority of union men belonged to decentralized craft unions bargaining mostly with small firms. Emotionally involved in their skilled work, they naturally sought out fellow craftsmen for both social and economic reasons, voluntarily joining with peers to protest when the employer made unfair demands or infringed on job rights. But a purely local union soon becomes an economic captive. An imperative of successful unionism is a necessity for *universality*. Most union benefits are collective goods going to all workers in the affected industry, craft, or market area. Unions cannot bargain for their members alone; their wage and other gains accrue to every worker similarly situated, union and nonunion alike. The union's opposition to "free riders" is well known from their crusade to expand the union shop, a device for forcing compulsory union membership.

The principles of unionism are, in this way, similar to the principles of government. Citizens may be allowed, probably indirectly, to vote on the issue of a tax increase, but once tax rates are set all citizens must pay, even those who are strongly opposed to the rate structure. Just so unions must organize all workers, else it will pay individuals to accept the benefits of union negotiations while avoiding the dues of union affiliation. Unions are commonly founded by political activists seeking only the correction of some economic grievance, but they must acquire at least the latent support of all affected workers, even if by involuntary means, for the organization to be permanently successful.

It is, of course, always difficult to secure the universal support of individuals for collective activities. This difficulty is minimized for craft unionists working in regionalized firms, for they need only organize a single craft in their area, providing that new firms and additional workers entering the area become unionized. But even craft unions must in time bolster their wage protection by binding the craft's entire national following, for when large numbers of skilled workers in the mobile American economy are outside the union fold, employers have a ready reserve of strike breakers.

For industrial unions, relying heavily on unskilled members, it is impossible to organize or control all potential job entrants. They must organize the whole firm, then the entire industry. It is not, as Selig Perlman wrote, the worker who is perpetually obsessed with job consciousness, but the unskilled worker's union.[4] There is a "universal imperative" stemming from the collective nature of union gains that forces industrial unions to control the job. Control of the job may not, during full employment, be a prime goal for the individual worker, but it is an organizational necessity for the industrial union. Only through job control can the industrial union hope to receive union dues for the dispensing of collective benefits. And the more jobs the industrial union controls, the greater its economic power.

Labor Unions in Key Industries

THE impressive achievements of unions bargaining with center firms during the postwar period is an indication of their relentless pursuit of the universality principle. They are, in addition, highly dependent on the contemporary phenomenon of center business control in key industries. We noted in Chapter 4 that a primary characteristic of key industries is high concentration. We also noted that key industries are, with small exception, largely dominated by center firms. During the postwar period, these center-controlled key industries have provided targets for mounting labor wage demands for several reasons.

1. Market Characteristics • Key industries are intertwined in an input-output nexus. Most rank among the largest customers of one or more brother key industries. The largest consumer of non-ferrous metals is the electrical industry; of rubber and electrical

---

4. The well-known theory of "job consciousness" is set forth in Selig Perlman, *Theory of the Labor Movement*, The Macmillan Company, 1928. Union benefits as collective goods are discussed in Mancur Olson, Jr., *The Logic of Collective Action*, Harvard University Press, 1965, Chapter III.

equipment and steel, the automobile industry; of aluminum, aircraft. Key industries also exhibit a high sensitivity to business fluctuations. This is to be expected, since one of our criteria in designating "key" industry was the production of capital goods. But the sales of key industries are more dependent on the level of aggregate demand than on small price variations. Their income-demand link is tighter than their price-demand link with incomes constant, or at least both management and labor *assume* this to be true. This fact, coupled with the center economy's oligopolistic preference for administered pricing, means that center firms in key industries can pass wage increases on to their customers through price rises when aggregate demand is climbing, but that prices tend to fall little when aggregate demand falters. Thus higher key-industry wages are easily provided by the firm during prosperity, yet the high wage levels can be maintained by the union during recession by accepting the alternative of unemployment.

Unions do accept the unemployment alternative to a wage cut during recessions because they cannot bargain with the firm over prices; they have no assurance that the firm will lower prices and *attempt* to increase output and employment *even if* the union accepts lower wage rates. Can anyone imagine a union leader negotiating a wage reduction with the hope that he can convince the membership that their falling wages will induce the firm to cut prices and stimulate demand and, consequently, employment? Undoubtedly most union members believe that changes in the contents of their pay packets have a desultory influence on the availability of work.

In most key industries neither management nor labor perceives a direct link between small wage increases and industry employment. Both regard outside factors as much more important in determining industrial output and employment.

2. *Geographic Proximity* • Key industry plants and offices are concentrated in Southern New England, the Middle Atlantic states, and the Southern Great Lakes area with a substantial subgroup in Southern California. For example, 98 percent of the members of the American Machine Tool Builders Association are

located in the Northeast-Midwest industrial heartland and half of the nonheartland members are in California. Although the geographic core of American industry comprises only 7.7 percent of the nation's area, it boasts 52 percent of the national income, 43 percent of the population, and 70 percent of U.S. industry.[5] Thus the key industries occupy a weakly linked labor market, located in regions where worker attitudes toward unionism are the most favorable.

3. Firm Size • Characterized by scale economies and controlled by center firms, key industries have both relatively large firms and plants. As a result, workers, remote from management, are more willing to join the union. Employee morale represents a constant threat to productivity, restraining management's willingness to undermine unionism. Large establishments also lend themselves to low-cost union recruitment.

4. Similarity of Production Process • High capital-output and capital-labor ratios are the rule in key industries which makes labor costs a relatively small portion of total cost. Mass and process production are far more prevalent inside the key group than elsewhere.

5. Common Pricing Behavior • Center firms in key industries rarely, if ever, price to maximize short-run profits. We have already mentioned the joint-cost problem discouraging such pricing for multiproduct firms. In addition, the long-run orientation of center firm management encourages pricing that may (1) bar or retard industry entry by new firms and (2) stimulate long-run increases in industry demand. Given imperfect knowledge of their product demand curves and the crude means by which oligopolists secure common prices, center firms are likely to operate on the inelastic portion of their demand curves, although this is contrary to the assumptions of conventional microeconomic theory. Thus center firms in key industries usually possess unexploited monopoly pricing power which they can use if unions in-

5. Edward L. Ullman, "Regional Development and the Geography of Concentration," in John Friedman and William Alonso (eds.), *Regional Development and Planning,* M. I. T. Press, 1964, p. 155.

crease their per unit wage costs. When this happens, unions in key industries can gain higher wages without suffering short-run employment losses, although the substitution of capital for labor may cut long-run employment.

6. *Concern with a Favorable Image* · Center firms are sensitive to both public and personnel relations. Productivity is always vulnerable to a fall in employee morale; this prompts center firms to be "good" employers. Consistently paying wages above the level required to clear the relevant labor market, they can hire the best of the available workers. One of the center firm's prime economic advantages lies in its ability to select both superior management and labor.

7. *Stable Industry Composition* · Because of significant barriers to industry entry, unions in key industries are less exposed to the danger of new, unorganized firms. Easy industry entry inevitably enlarges the potential nonunion sector, increasing organizing costs and decreasing union universality. Plant mobility poses a major threat to unions, since organized plants often move outside the union-oriented geographic core into the union-resistant South. When compared with periphery manufacturing, key industry plants are relatively immobile.

In brief, American key industries provide an ideal setting for labor union initiative. Their interdependence makes a strike in any key sector critical to others in the key nexus. Geographic proximity and common skill needs tie key industries to a joint labor market. The prevalence of large firms provides organizing economies of scale, strengthens the workers' propensity to unionize, creates a morale-productivity problem for management, and places the firm's personnel relations in the public eye. Capital-intensive production reduces the per unit impact of wage increases, while administered pricing makes it possible to pass wage increases to buyers without cutting employment when demand is high. Both management and labor consider employment the handmaiden of aggregate demand but only distantly related to wage levels.

Pattern Bargaining

THE UNION RESPONSE to this fortunate convergence of factors in key industries during the generally prosperous postwar period has been *pattern bargaining*.[6] Since 1948, wages and fringe benefits won from key industry employers have moved upward at an almost identical rate. Most key product prices have fallen little if at all since World War II, allowing the wage pattern to ascend without interruption. Labor participation in key industry bargaining is highly organized. Most of the involved unions are former members of the CIO, now merged with the AFL. They have a well-established means of communication. Pattern-setting wage negotiations fall into relatively short periods, ranging from one to four years.

If center firms gain their financial strength by "exploiting" their customers, this power over price also fortifies labor in the center. All center wage boosts between 1957 and 1962 were monopolistic if we define any real wage increase as monopolistic when got from collective bargaining with qualified applicants unemployed. The decline in production worker employment in, for example, the steel industry, indicates that numerous workers were willing individually to accept employment at rates below the bargained rate. Eckstein and Fromm link the rapid rise in steel prices during the 1950's to "an extraordinary rise in wages which is the result of bargaining between a strong union and a management with strong market power in the product market."[7] But as steel wages go, so go wage gains in automobiles, aluminum, farm machinery, electrical equipment, rubber, copper, aircraft, petroleum refining, shipbuilding, industrial chemicals—in short, with minor exception, the entire key industry segment of the center economy.

Furthermore, the wage elevation within key industries exercised a considerable spillover effect on other manufacturing,

6. The two best studies of postwar pattern bargaining are John E. Maher, "The Wage Pattern in the United States, 1946–1957," *Industrial and Labor Relations Review*, Vol. 15, No. 1 (October, 1961); and Otto Eckstein and Thomas A. Wilson, "The Determination of Money Wages in American Industry," *Quarterly Journal of Economics*, Vol. LXXVI, No. 3 (August, 1962).

7. Otto Eckstein and Gary Fromm, *Steel and the Postwar Inflation*, Study Paper No. 2, Study of Employment, Growth and Price Levels, Joint Economic Committee (1959), p. 34.

and even beyond. On the whole, nonkey manufacturing is not so well organized, has lower wages, is more geographically dispersed, and shows fewer input-output ties than key industries, yet the uniform success of labor in key industries spreads a wage-inflating current throughout manufacturing. Key industry unions provided the first wedge to industrial wage pressures throughout the economy.

The pattern setting bargainers of center business and center labor act as *central bargainers* for the entire manufacturing economy, with ramifications that extend ultimately into the most remote periphery corner. The perennial negotiations conducted by these central bargainers is perhaps the closest approach to nongovernmental centralized planning now allowed under American capitalism. Wage gains in one key industry are sparely diluted in other key sectors, and their upward motion is soon transferred to the less prominent members of the manufacturing fraternity. When wages rise, prices soon follow, almost at the same time. And manufacturing price increases cannot but affect investment and pricing decisions in agriculture, transportation, and other sectors of the economy. The impact of central bargaining loses momentum as it ripples from manufacturing to other areas, but it exercises an impact on the entire economic structure before it is spent.

Such influential proceedings are not conducted without the appropriate ceremony. They have for some time aroused political interest in Washington, dating at least from President Cleveland's dispatching of troops to Chicago in 1894 to put down the American Railway Union's strike against the Pullman Company. In the postwar period steel industry negotiations and pricing policies in particular have prompted governmental intervention. In 1952 President Truman felt compelled by the Korean War to seize the steel industry, releasing control only upon an edict from the Supreme Court. President Eisenhower designated Vice-President Nixon as his representative through the four-month steel strike of 1959, ending in a settlement on January 4, 1960.

The 1965 steel contract negotiations followed the postwar pattern, by then firmly entrenched. Meetings between labor and management negotiators begun in the winter proved fruitless. As the strike deadline approached, the President asked both parties to agree to an extension of the announced strike date. The post-deadline talks were moved from Pittsburgh, the home of the industry, to the White House. The secretaries of Labor and Commerce and the chairman of the Council of Economic Advisers assumed major roles in the hitherto deadlocked proceedings. On September 3, just before the Labor Day weekend, President Johnson announced on television a settlement to an expectant nation. The United Steelworkers had gained another real wage boost although their compensation without the latest increment ran a third above the general factory average. The pattern remained intact.

Pattern bargaining with Federal sanction and participation has regional side effects. As center firms broadcast their plants somewhat more generously about the countryside, and as the nation draws itself into a single labor market, pattern bargaining encourages uniform wage rates regardless of location. Fringe benefits are equalized more readily than money wages, and traditional geographical differentials are nibbled to death rather than devoured in a single gulp, yet the reduction of regional disparities has continued since World War II.

The Federal government is a silent partner in pattern bargaining. In addition to its obvious role in maintaining union security (under the National Labor Relations Act) and serving as the arbitrator of last, and perhaps inevitable, resort, the government strives to create a favorable economic environment. Negotiated wage uniformity is more extensive during periods of prosperity and mild inflation than recession and depression for two reasons: (1) cost of living increases affect all workers, generating widespread pressures by labor for relief, and (2) during periods of adequate business profit, differences in corporate ability to pay do not obstruct uniform wage adjustments. Thus by boosting the economy toward full employment, the Federal government allows the private wage policy set by the central bargainers to exercise its upward influence without a negating interruption.

The union's drive for industrial wage parity in key industries is hindered by one major stumbling block—the survival of periphery economy elements. Loyal opposition firms create one pattern-bargaining problem. If the loyal opposition is less efficient than its center competitors, as is often the case, pattern wages may drive the firm out of business, unemploying many union members. Organized labor often feels obliged to grant the periphery relief from wage patterns. But to do so weakens the union's position. Top union officials must perspicaciously consider the distribution of employment between firms within an industry, constantly deflecting a shift of production from efficient to less efficient firms unable to meet the wage pattern. Labor is thus reluctant to undermine the industry standard. They willingly aid the loyal opposition's attempts to increase efficiency, but should these attempts prove insufficient, loyal opposition demise is usually accepted by the union without regret. The price-shaving propensities of loyal opposition competitors cuts into the union's economic power.

A second impediment to labor objectives in key industries is presented by backward satellites. The jurisdiction of center labor commonly extends beyond the corporate bounds of center business and its loyal opposition into the industry's suppliers. As we saw in Chapter 6, backward satellites are forced into a simulated perfect competition. This downward pressure on satellite prices may require labor to grant wage relief to the satellites, breaking the industry pattern. In this special case, the interests of big labor and big business collide, establishing a countervailing power.[8] The problem is most critical in the automobile industry, where the United Auto Workers want a congressional hearing on monopsony with the hope of eventually securing relief for auto industry suppliers from satellitic profit constraints.[9] When the interests of central bargainers in key industries collide, a high priority economic problem arises which government finds difficult to ignore. In this instance big labor may well countervail effectively on behalf of specific small periphery enterprises.

A third dilemma confronting center labor bargainers resides in the international economy. To the extent that U.S. wage gains

8. John Kenneth Galbraith, *American Capitalism* (Sentry Edition), Houghton Mifflin Company, 1962.
9. *Business Week* (July 24, 1965), pp. 43–44.

exceed increases in domestic labor productivity, foreign suppliers of key industry products become more attractive. The strategic importance of key industry outputs retards this import-substitution effect, providing a margin of domestic wage protection. Two economists discovered that independent steel fabricators in the U.S. continued to buy half their wire rod from domestic producers at prices above those charged by importers.[10] But such protection from foreign competitors is not uniform among key industries nor is it a reliable foundation for permanent wage patterns.

Finally, the migration of center firms to other nations, principally the European Common Market countries, poses a labor threat. Foreign workers are now outside the domain of American center bargainers. Should their wage rates and productivity combine to give the foreign facilities of American center firms substantially lower unit costs, it might well pay American firms to produce overseas for their American markets. Should the continuing tariff negotiations between the U.S. and the Common Market countries successfully lower or eliminate trade barriers, the threat of foreign production by American firms for the U.S. market could become very real.

How Unions Aid the Center Economy

BUT were it not for center labor membership spillovers into the periphery economy and international complications, contemporary relations between central bargainers would at worst be a lover's quarrel. Key industry unions provide a useful prop to center economy stability. This center economy support takes at least four forms.

1) UNIFORMITY OF WAGE RATES. Center unions put pressure on key industry competitors to pay uniform wage rates, including loyal opposition and potential center firm competitors. Pattern wages remove wage competition from the center economy, making an additional entry barrier to new, poorly financed competitors.

10. Walter Adams and J. B. Dirlam, "Steel Imports and Vertical Oligopoly Power," *American Economic Review*, Vol. 54 (September, 1964), p. 645.

2) SECURITY FROM UNAUTHORIZED LABOR UNREST. In return for high wages, center firms are granted protection from unauthorized labor unrest. Unions give an orderly grievance procedure for individual gripes and suppress wildcat strikes when local groups show discontent. One UAW official recently complained, "What are we here for? To maintain a docile labor force by seeing that people get enough in the way of wages and fringe benefits and finally go to the grave well-fed and content? Life consists of more than that." [11] His fellow unionists probably agree, but most have learned by now to seek life's other meanings outside the union hall.

3) INSURANCE AGAINST GOVERNMENT INTERVENTION IN THE AREA OF WAGES AND CONDITIONS OF LABOR. The combined political power of center labor and center business makes it difficult for government to assume more than voluntary last minute arbitration. Informal Presidential intervention is expected and probably welcomed by both parties in pattern-setting disputes, but the President and his representatives now act more like marriage counselors than judges. By peaceably settling their differences and providing the President with a politically favorable image of peacemaker, both parties augment their intangible political capital in the White House. The appeal of the present system of resolving center labor disputes over any other system involving government led *Fortune* magazine to proclaim that "Labor Unions Are Worth the Price." [12]

4) KNOWN WAGE RATES. Collective bargaining gives center firms known wage rates during the life of the contract, preventing unplanned wage increases during periods of labor scarcity and thus facilitating corporate planning.

Yet just when the common-law marriage of center business and center labor seems to be working well, when the two parties have made a mutually satisfactory accommodation, sanctified by Presidential authority and often consummated in the White House, large numbers of impartial observers are agreeing that the state of the unions is unhealthy, that collective bargaining is

11. Center for the Study of Democratic Institutions, *op. cit.*, p. 24.
12. *Fortune*, Vol. LXVII, No. 5 (May, 1963).

old before its time. Can it be that success has spoiled key industry labor?

The Future of Center Labor

CENTER LABOR in key industries may well be the long-run victim of short-run victories. Rising wage costs increase management's propensity to substitute physical capital and its complementary factor, human capital, for labor. Using steel as an example, we find that expensive wage and fringe benefits plus pressure from foreign producers and competitive materials—aluminum, plastics, concrete—are spurring the industry to an extensive modernization program. Already the ratio of white-collar to blue-collar jobs has risen in steel from one in nine in 1934 to one in four during 1964. The United Steelworkers are resigned to continued long-term shrinkage in its core membership in basic steel.

Although the steelworkers, like other central bargaining unions, hope to grow by organizing the unorganized, the environment for future union growth is hostile. Center firms with easily unionized plants are now highly organized. The remainder of U.S. manufacturing capacity is geographically dispersed and composed of smaller plants. White-collar workers, especially the professional group, are not attracted by labor union goals. Professionals do not pursue money gains as their first goal, but rather they seek professional recognition. They march to the beat of professional mores, even when doing so involves economic sacrifice. As professional workers grow in workforce importance, there comes a general diminution in the power of raw money incentives. About one U.S. worker in eight now has professional status, and is beyond the reach of contemporary labor unions.

There are still millions of poorly paid workers in the periphery economy, but periphery firms do not offer the wage opportunities of the center. Where profit margins are tight, a close connection exists between wages and employment; the periphery firm's ability to pay severely limits pattern bargaining possibilities. There is, no doubt, considerable truth to the indictment voiced by a UAW leader:

As a matter of fact, isn't there a slight tendency on our part as a labor organization not to want to bother with certain people because it is beneath our dignity as staff representatives to sign a contract with a $1.35 wage rate in it? Aren't we a little ashamed to have people know that we associate with that sort of agreement? This is one of the things that has made Hoffa successful. He will go out and organize car-washers and negotiate a contract for $1.25 an hour, whereas we have a tendency to look only at those who are making $3 or $4 an hour so that we can have some pride in the type of agreement we negotiate. We have been forgetting the guy way down below who is really getting kicked in the face. Nobody is doing anything about him except Hoffa.[13]

The Teamsters Union, with over 1,700,000 members, is the nation's largest. Teamsters membership lies mostly in trucking, but its 350,000 membership in industrial plants gives it considerable strength among factory workers. Teamster officials stress areawide and industrywide bargaining, claiming that all workers, without limitation, fall within their jurisdiction. The Teamsters' organizational base in trucking makes them unique. While largely outside manufacturing, the trucking industry is critical to it, forming the transportation link between center firms. Although essential to center economy operations, the trucking industry retains a small-firm, competitive, periphery orientation. In short, the major coordinating force in the critical trucking sector is the Teamsters Union.

Jimmy Hoffa's ambition to create a central bargaining type union in a periphery-oriented industry reminds one of an earlier labor union coordinator in transportation, Eugene V. Debs. Was the railroad industry in the 1890's, and is the trucking industry today, a suitable environment for the same style of centralized bargaining characteristic of key industries? Railroading was, at the turn of the century, a flourishing industry dominated by a few major firms, but it proved not to have the technological nor managerial potential of the contemporary center economy. The techniques of staff-and-line management, later adopted by most

13. Center for the Study of Democratic Institutions, *op. cit.*, pp. 29–30.

center firms, were pioneered by the railroads, and, in their day, railroad corporations had abundant financial resources. But the railroad giants did not follow the pull of technology, did not develop the institutional flexibility that would have enabled them to shift their talents from the industry when its lush days were gone.

Nor do today's trucking firms seem capable of spawning a new technically oriented center family. Thus trucking cannot, without adopting the business style of center firms, support Jimmy Hoffa's ambitions. Trucking as we know it may be no more than a temporary phase in the transportation revolution. Unless center-style firms organize all transportation systems, the long-run threat of technological change hovers over the Teamsters' trucking base. Unlike most earlier unions, the Teamsters now seek diversification with a vengeance. Perhaps time will tell whether diversification can aid large unions as much as large firms.

Union growth by diversification encounters the now familiar obstacles to labor expansion. Most women consider themselves short-timers in the labor force and resist unionization; yet women continue to increase their numbers in the world of work. White-collar employees, rapidly expanding their number, identify most often with management, not labor. The industrializing South remains nonunion territory because of the national union's stand on civil rights and the overwhelming rural backgrounds and attitudes of workers. Only time can erode the anti-organizational bias of workers who have left behind the countryside but not parochial attitudes.

We can summarize the causes of center labor membership stagnation and center business prosperity during the postwar period by dividing what employees sell into two categories— *labor power* and *human capital*. Labor power is sold by those who perform tasks susceptible to capital substitution. If a technically feasible machine can do your job, you are selling labor power. Your collar may be white and neither your wages nor the size of the market may justify capital substitution. But if you are a candidate for technological unemployment by known capital-intensive techniques, you provide labor power.

If your employment is complementary to that of the most

technically advanced physical capital, you trade human capital for the contents of your pay packet. Human capital, like physical capital, is man-made and reproducible. Its regenerative industry is the education sector, a key locale for labor transformation, where human capital is both the output and the most important input. Like machine tools, human capital propagates itself by consuming its own product.

When economies industrialize, they expand their physical capital and its complement, human capital. As the economy reaches industrial maturity, both kinds of capital become more abundant and increasingly sophisticated. To give one crude measure of the growth of human capital in the United States, persons twenty-five years and older had, in 1940, completed a median of 8.6 years of schooling. By 1950 the median had risen to 9.3; by 1960, 10.6. Since 1940 the proportion of workers age eighteen to sixty-four with four or more years of secondary school had risen from 32 to 57 percent, and these gains have not been restricted to younger workers.

The vaulting demand for human capital, accompanied by a significant increase in the rate of human capital accumulation, is reshaping today's labor markets. Center business firms are aligning their operations with this shift to capital, securing their future and making themselves indispensable to the U.S. economy. But organized labor, even that in the center economy, continues to find its membership strength among those who supply labor power. Now that central bargaining unions have securely established a place for themselves in the center economy, even though on a declining membership base, they are becoming just another vested interest group.

Unions, now established in the key industry segment of the center economy, are beneficiaries of oligopoly pricing. Center firms have all but ceased their earlier attempts to dislodge the unions; they are, in fact, beginning to embrace union wage pacts in preference to the potentially more harmful wage determination by government guidelines. Labor radicalism, spawned by its past struggle for survival, now lingers as but a quaint remnant adding occasional color to the bourgeois pronouncements of today's labor statesmen. The rousing oratory of yesterday's agita-

tors can still be found, but it puts only temporary fire under contemporary labor audiences. Our new folk songs are an outgrowth
of the civil rights' movement, not worker protest.

Cumulative collective bargaining has ameliorated the central
issues formerly dividing labor and management in the center
economy—grievance procedures, union security, adequate pensions, supplementary unemployment benefits. [PAUL JACOBS, economist, University of California, Berkeley — *We also have to realize
that new union members are coming in at a time when the union
has already taken care of their working conditions. They don't
know what it was like before there was a union shop and before
workers were protected by agreements and arbitration. They
not only don't know but they don't care to be educated on labor
history.*][14] To secure further advances, labor turns to government where, in politics as in collective bargaining, the art of
the possible prevails. The old militancy is incompatible with the
new society of cooperation and compromise. Hostile employers
and militant unionists can still be found, but they are most often
partitioned into the small-scale fringes of the economy. [JACOBS
— *When workers see their leaders getting more and more isolated from them, they begin to adopt the attitude of, what the
hell, it's a big company and it's a big union—they're both squeez-
ing us simultaneously and we're caught in the middle.*][15]

Social Implications of Pattern Bargaining

WHAT IS the import of center economy bargaining for the U.S.
economy as a whole? The most obvious long-run consequence
is the encouragement that an unabating wage pressure lends to
the substitution of capital, human and physical, for labor. Center
unions have made rising labor costs a high priority threat to the
maintenance of long-run cost constancy, inducing managements
to allocate a major portion of their energy and finances to the deflation of unit labor costs. The scientific community has enormous potential for displacing labor power, and union wage
agitations are providing part of the impetus necessary to transform this potentiality into actuality.

14. *Ibid.*, p. 7.
15. *Ibid.*

In addition, across-the-board settlements typical of the center economy are narrowing the differential between skilled and unskilled labor, fostering the employment of the skilled but truncating the employment of the unskilled when the economy is slack. Bargaining emphasis on fringe benefits also promotes the utilization of skilled employees with high productivity. Most center plants are composed of a nucleus of senior hands serving their employers like industrial family retainers, assisted during periods of high demand by a floating crew of transients. In recessions the less-experienced transients are pushed into the periphery economy or into unemployment.

The creation by center labor and management of a private welfare state in key industries is eroding the employability of the transient group, making it less expensive to pay the nucleus workers overtime than to bring additional workers under the welfare umbrella. Since the nucleus is the backbone of organized labor, they naturally seek their own interests through the union, reinforcing the pattern of overemployment accompanied by unemployment. As automation continues in center plants, the union reaction is to preserve the status of the nucleus through gradual reductions in employment when demand is low, leaving the transients to longer periods of unemployment or eventual banishment to the periphery economy.

No economist bemoans the necessity for labor mobility; the professional applauds the transfer of labor from key industries when it is no longer needed there. The provision of services is one specialty of the periphery economy, and the demand for services should continue to grow as population and affluence increase. If pattern bargaining in the center economy has kept manufacturing wages high and encouraged factor substitution, this very capital intensity has promoted increases in manufacturing labor productivity. Surely an increase in productivity cannot be lamented, no matter what its impetus. What is often overlooked is that the juxtaposition of managerial talent, inexpensive capital funds, and high wages has resulted in a disproportionate allocation of human capital to the center economy, just as the Federal government's massive defense expenditures have concentrated much of our scientific capability in defense industries.

It is an economic cliché that productivity gains are more difficult in services than in goods production, but the proposition is yet to be tested by giving both sectors equal access to technical and financial resources. Given the limited supply of top technical personnel remaining after the Federally financed defense effort is taken care of, it is small wonder that periphery economy activities yield small productivity gains.

The much heralded shift, then, of production labor from the center economy and key industries marks a new period in American labor history. For the first time, shifts in production techniques and demand are exerting a pressure on labor power *contrary* to the pull of wages. The traditional shift of labor in American history has been from the low-wage, low-productivity agricultural sector to the higher-wage, higher-productivity industrial sector, especially into manufacturing. But the agricultural labor push is of declining absolute importance and the number of potential rural migrants is decreasing.[16]

The second stage of labor shift is from manufacturing to services, trade, and government. These sectors accounted for over four-fifths of the increase in nonagricultural employment between 1948 and 1960, with much of this expansion occurring in the ranks of professional, technical, and other white-collar labor. From 1948 to 1960, the strong centers of U.S. unionism—durable-goods manufacturing, transportation, mining, and construction—increased wages more rapidly than did the trade and service sectors.[17]

But while manufacturing wages continue to rise, manufacturing employment has fallen into relative decline. Employment in manufacturing almost doubled from the turn of the century to 1929, growing more rapidly than the population. From 1929 to 1940, manufacturing employment was virtually constant, while population rose 10 percent and output expanded by 20 percent. Since 1947, manufacturing employees have increased only

16. The shift of labor power from high to low wage sectors is discussed in Lloyd Ulman, "Labor Mobility and the Industrial Wage Structure in the Postwar United States, "*Quarterly Journal of Economics,* Vol. LXXIX, (February, 1965), pp. 73-97.

17. Lowell E. Gallaway, "Labor Mobility, Resource Allocation, and Structural Unemployment," *American Economic Review,* Vol. 53 (September, 1963), pp. 694–716.

one half as fast as population, but one-fifth as rapidly as output. Had it not been for the artificial stimulant originating in the American war efforts, hot and cold, the full impact of manufacturing's relative decline would have been fully evident for the last quarter century. Only wars and rumors of wars have kept the demand for industrial labor intermittently buoyant during the last generation.

As the American economy moves further along the path to industrial maturity, even limited wars may prove insufficient to maintain manufacturing employment against the erosion of secular trends. Perhaps the Great Society will provide a governmental net just in time to catch the tumbling labor power from the center economy, stepping up the conversion of labor power to human capital. Certainly a Great Society would give more stability and greater welfare than the temporary relief from secular forces inspired by the great wars.

8. Government as an Industrial Organization

No SIGNIFICANT AREA OF American economic life is untouched by the actions of government. To name but a few of government's more important functions it acts as a seller of services (post office, government printing office); a buyer of products (customized defense items, homogeneous agricultural products); a subsidizer of economic sectors (agriculture, transportation); a regulator of firms (public utility regulation, antitrust prosecution); a provider of collective goods (defense, education); an underwriter of minimum welfare (unemployment compensation, direct relief, social security); and the overseer of aggregate economic activity (monetary policy, fiscal policy).

Economic problems or goals can be divided into three groups: the microeconomic goals of correct resource allocation and economic efficiency, the macroeconomic goal of maintaining full employment, and the long-run goal of economic growth. The American government plays a major part in fostering all three. We shall begin by discussing government as a microeconomic force, moving then to government's macroeconomic role, and finally we shall consider government's influence on the maintenance of economic growth in the long run.

Businessmen have traditionally viewed government as a form of business, a major enterprise that should be operated according to sound business principles. This limited interpretation of government has come under sustained and largely successful attack from the liberal community during the past generation, and justly so. Yet we should not lose sight of the grain of truth in this older doctrine. Government does, in a few important respects, closely resemble a very large firm. It can be meaningfully interpreted as an enterprise existing to meet the demand for public services at a cost approximately covered by its revenue at full employment. The critical term in this definition is, of course, full employment. With the Employment Act of 1946, the United States government officially declared its major macroeconomic goal to be the promotion of "maximum employment, production, and purchasing power." Until this goal is reached, the equating of government costs and revenues must wait; but like firms, large and small, the government continues to have costs and revenues, and their mutual relationship must not be ignored.

Although we often speak of "government" as though it were a single entity, the American system actually embraces a multitude of governments—one Federal, fifty state governments, and countless local units. Like a large multiproduct, decentralized center firm, all of these governmental bodies are linked together through financial and administrative ties culminating in the Federal hub. Through the use of Federal grants-in-aid or matching-funds programs, state and local governments perform their services within general administrative guidelines devised in Washington. Practicing decentralization without abdication, the Federal government acts as staff management, leaving most of the line decisions to smaller governmental units.

The division of governmental decision making into staff-and-line duties has not evolved without public controversy. Yet the general pattern is deeply etched. Various public officials, many of them at the state level, periodically voice their concern about the usurping of "states' rights," yet few states seem equally concerned about the rights of their own hostages, the city and county governments. The states are, in general, far less liberal in granting their own subdivisions local autonomy than is the Federal government. Unlike center firms, where control is substantially free from interference by owners, government officials at all levels must remain sensitive to public sentiment. Thus one hears the most frequent complaints about states' rights violations when the voters of a state are in disagreement with broad areas of Federal policy. But coordinated decentralization seems equally well-established in the most progressive center firms and in American government.

Like most center firms, government is a high fixed cost concern. Costs do not fall appreciably in the public sector during temporary declines in national income and government revenue, for the variable cost component of most public facilities and services is comparatively low. Most studies show that government, at both the Federal and lower levels, is a constant or decreasing cost industry. The postal service, for example, has experienced decreasing long-run average costs.[1] And the most important state and local government services—education, police and fire protection, refuse collection—accounting for 80 to 85 percent of sub-Federal expenditures, show, in general, constant long-run costs. Water and sewerage services, accounting for 8 to 10 percent of local expenditures, show falling costs to scale.[2]

In addition, government operations, like those in center firms, depend on the generous use of human capital. Professional and technical personnel comprise the largest component of government employees. About one in every three persons recently trained in a professional field works directly for government.[3] Since human capital, from staff management to technicians, is a scarce economic factor, the government directly controls the allocation of a large share of one of the economy's most precious resources.

As we noted in Chapter 2, the ultimate center firm objective is survival. No center management wants to preside over the interment of a great corporation. And a major corporate weapon against firm demise is the center link with technical progress.

1. Morton S. Baratz, "Cost Behavior and Pricing Policy in the Post Office," *Land Economics,* Vol. XXXVIII (November, 1962); reprinted in Donald S. Watson, *Price Theory in Action,* Houghton Mifflin Company, 1965.
2. Werner Z. Hirsch, "Expenditure Implications of Metropolitan Growth and Consolidations," *Review of Economics and Statistics,* Vol. XLI, No. 3 (August, 1959), pp. 232–241.
3. Eli Ginzberg, Dale L. Hiestand, and Beatrice G. Reubens, *The Pluralistic Economy,* McGraw-Hill, Inc., 1965, p. 122.

So long as technical change exerts its force *through* center firms and not *against* them, they have neutralized their most potent long-run threat. Government in the United States is subject to no internal threat to continued survival, but its mortality is challenged from abroad. It is in the area of national defense that government pursues technological progress with supreme vigor. The progress of American military technology ("dirty science") has been so rapid as to transform completely the rules of the international survival game just as, on a smaller scale, the rules of classical competition have been overrun by progressive center firms.

Perhaps the most important similarity between the government, particularly the Federal apex, and the center economy is their community of interest in prosperity. Since the Federal government garners the majority of its revenue from a reasonably progressive income tax, any increase in national income will yield a considerable return to the Federal treasury. So significant is this growth in Federal revenue as the economy rises toward full employment that it has been given an official name, the high-employment surplus. Thus a movement toward full employment increases the Federal government's discretionary income (funds above the nominal commitment to on-going programs), allowing *either* new and expanded expenditures *or* reduced tax rates, or some combination of both. Prosperity presents Federal officials with happy alternatives.

All business firms benefit from prosperity, but like many good things, a business upturn spreads its blessings unevenly throughout the business community. Center firms, being larger, more dispersed, and better diversified, increase their prosperity cash flows more readily than periphery firms. A business boom immediately boosts one of the touchstones of center business superiority, financial strength. While most enterprises enlarge their solvency during an economic recovery, center firms realize the greatest return in liquidity. To those who have, in a business revival, more is given. Center economy membership is not fixed, and prosperity allows several enterprises on the center threshold to enter the abundant economy. But the tension between center and periphery, already skewed in the center economy's direction, begins, during a business revival, to intensify the center's advantage. This complementarity of center and Federal revenue advantage touches on government's macroactivities, and we shall have more to say about that shortly.

Government differs, of course, from the center economy in numerous ways. Public bodies cannot depend on advertising to mold the demand for their products. They forgo a major center firm weapon. At least one economist contends that the government's silence about the valuable services it offers explains in part the public sector's starvation on the local level during periods of private abundance.[4]

Government also differs from center firms in its emphasis on good will. Public relations are important to center firms, but they are the essence of successful government. As a result, the Federal government will at times lower its prices (taxes), as it did during 1964, but hesitates to increase tax rates even during peacetime prosperity, making Federal tax rates sticky in an upward direction, except during periods of major military involvement. Center firms, on the other hand, are slow to lower prices but quick to increase them.

The Federal Government as an Economic Center

As a microeconomic force the Federal government acts for a few industries, the most prominent examples being the defense industries and agriculture, like a center economy, converting dependent firms into satellites. A host of relatively small service enterprises, located mainly in Washington, operate as satellites to government agencies. For example, several law firms, boasting such famous public policy lawyers as Dean Acheson, Thomas G. Corcoran, Earl Kintner, Clark Clifford, Stephen Ailes, Thurman Arnold, and Paul A. Porter, prosper by advising businessmen, particularly center businessmen, in their dealings with government.

In the two major industries—defense and agriculture—where government serves as the prime buyer, government suppliers

4. Wilbur Thompson, *A Preface to Urban Economics,* The Johns Hopkins Press, 1965, p. 269.

face a demand situation like that confronting the center economy's backward satellites. Prices and product specifications are determined by the large public buyer; technical changes originate in, or are financed by the government. But there are important differences. Government does not, in general, try to force its satellites into a condition of contrived perfect competition. In the case of agriculture, any attempt to do so would negate the government's purpose in serving as a major buyer.

An outstanding characteristic of the U.S. government's two principal satellitic industries is a very rapid rate of technical progress. This rapidity of technical change is reflected in the employment and input mix of both industries. In the aircraft industry, for example, nine of every ten employees were production workers at the height of World War II. By the Korean War, only seven of ten workers were directly engaged in production. By 1959, production workers, as a percent of total aircraft employment, fell below 50 percent. At present the aircraft employment mix is 12 percent management, 25 percent technical workers, 23 percent white-collar, and 40 percent production workers.[5]

The shift in agricultural factor inputs is equally dramatic. Between 1940 and 1958, the output of American farms increased 51 percent, while conventional inputs rose only 4 percent. In the eighteen years prior to 1959, the input of agricultural labor declined by one-half, while machinery and mechanical power use grew by 136 percent, fertilizer and lime consumption by 245 percent. Land and building inputs increased by only 8 percent.[6] As late as 1940, 66 percent of agricultural inputs were land and farm-resident labor. By 1961, these two farmer-owned factors were down to a 37 percent contribution. Nonfarm inputs almost doubled their proportionate share, growing from 34 to 63 percent.[7] The cost of farm chemicals alone now totals 10 percent of the farmer's cash outlay. In short, where the Federal government performs the center function, realized technical

5. Ginzberg, Hiestand, and Reubens, *op. cit.*, p. 153.
6. Dale E. Hathaway, *Government and Agriculture*, Macmillian, 1963, p. 92.
7. Harold F. Breimyer, "The Changing Industrial Organization," in L. B. Fletcher (ed.), *Farmers in the Market Economy*, Iowa State University Press, 1964, p. 157.

potential corrodes employment opportunities for labor power. Federal involvement in agriculture is peculiarly suggestive. Agriculture is the best example of an industry experiencing sustained governmental involvement over a long period. As such, perhaps an examination of agricultural trends and structure will help illuminate the impact of government acting as a simulated economic center.

Government and Agriculture: A Public Center with Private Periphery

FOR MOST American farmers, agriculture is still a way of life; for economists, it is a case study. Textbooks of beginning economics usually portray agriculture as an example of perfect competition, or at least as our best real-world specimen of that rarefied market form. True, farmers are plagued by production problems not characteristic of other industries, no matter how competitive, including extreme price instability and unstable, often pernicious, weather. But farmers are the archetypal price takers. They cannot sell above the going price, nor can they, by their individual actions, influence that price. Add to this the secular decline in demand for most farm products relative to industrial goods, the price and income inelasticity of demand for the majority of agricultural outputs *at the farm level*, the rapid advances in agricultural productivity coupled with inadequate movement out of farming, and you have the American farm problem as conventionally depicted.

There can be no doubt that agriculture is well suited for illustrating perfect competition in operation. The large number of competing firms (farms), homogeneous products, low average profits, and a dearth of agricultural advertising all conform to the neoclassical theorist's favorite market structure. But for us, American agriculture will serve to illustrate not so much the trials of a price taker as the vicissitudes of an industry with a lingering periphery-type orientation undergoing rapid technological change, considerable encroachment from the center economy, and partial domination by the Federal government.

American agriculture manifests much of the familiar duality

we found so tenacious in industry. As one noted economist observed:

> This country has in fact not one agriculture but two: an efficient, capital-intensive, commercial agriculture, located for the most part in the Middle West, Texas, and California, together with parts of the South; and a subsistence, labor-intensive, impoverished agriculture, largely in the South, in the hills of the border states, and in parts of New England.[8]

Yet this efficient, capital-intensive agriculture is not an agrarian replica of the industrial center. While large in agricultural terms, few big farms stand higher than pygmies when compared with the assets, sales, and employment of leading center firms. Nor does their internal structure follow the typical center pattern. Even sizable farms are poorly diversified and limited to a single geographic region. Most have not yet evolved out of the family-owned and managed stage; about 70 percent of American farm production comes from family farms. We are, in fact, developing a hereditary class of land-owning family farmers.[9] Virtually no American farms have international economic contacts, and, most important, agriculture is not often horizontally or vertically integrated.

But in agriculture, as in industry, size is very important. Large farms are, in general, highly productive, small ones are not. Only 8.3 percent of all U.S. farms make yearly sales of $20,000 or more, but these account for half of American agricultural production. And the most productive 3 percent of U.S. farms outproduce the lowest 78 percent.[10] During 1963, 91 percent of our total agricultural output was grown on 44 percent of our farms.[11] As a determinant of productivity, economic size is nowhere more important than in agriculture. Yet in many aspects the large, superproductive farm has more in common

8. Charles P. Kindleberger, *Economic Development* (Second Edition), McGraw-Hill, Inc., 1965, p. 176.

9. Don Paarlberg, *American Farm Policy*, John Wiley & Sons, Inc., 1964, p. 48.

10. Edward Higbee, *Farms and Farmers in an Urban Age*, The Twentieth Century Fund, 1963, pp. 50–51.

11. Willard W. Cochrane, *The City Man's Guide to the Farm Problem*, University of Minnesota Press, 1965, pp. 13–14.

with its small agricultural counterpart than with its size equivalent in industry.

All farms, large and small, sell inherently homogeneous commodities. In agriculture, the graded quality of the product means much, the source very little. In their commercial operations, almost all farmers are specialists. They produce a single cash crop, or at most two or three. Being price takers, every commercial farmer is a devoted cost cutter. Having no control over their price, farmers widen their profit margins through reducing costs. In short, American agriculture, productive and unproductive alike, inhabits a universe with an essentially periphery structure.

The agrobusiness enterprise in the United States includes much more than farming and ranching. Our vast agricultural complex falls into four distinct sectors: a factor supply sector, producing and distributing farm inputs; the farm plant, combining land, labor, capital, and management to produce a food and fiber output; the agricultural marketing system, processing and marketing farm products; and the government sector, underwriting the entire operation.

Although the farm plant operates under a periphery orientation, its suppliers and buyers do not. The factor supply sector is composed of farm machinery, a key industry dominated by three center firms; agricultural chemical companies, another key industry under center management; scattered farmers' supply cooperatives, distributing fuel, feed, fertilizer, and seed; and an assortment of free-agent service firms—bankers, lawyers, veterinarians, etc. During 1963, farmers purchased well over $15 billion worth of goods and services from these sources.[12] The agricultural marketing system is, in value terms, triple the size of the farm plant. Much of the marketing network is organized by center firms (large grocery retailers and their satellite food processors, major meat packers), while other segments are moving toward economic concentration (for example, the once-dispersed dairying industry); few farmers still rely on periphery marketing.

Government, the pivotal agricultural participant, brings a mix of services including research, education, regulation, and

12. *Ibid.*, p. 6.

financial and income support. The current annual cost of Federal activities in agriculture averages about $8.5 billion. Agricultural economists estimate that net farm income would fall about 50 percent in a few years if all commodity price and income support programs were eliminated.

Through the early 1960's, government price supports covered a variety of agricultural products, including wheat, cotton, corn, rice, peanuts, tobacco, oats, rye, barley, soybeans, and wool. When private buyers were not available at prices set by the government, farmers could sell their products to a government agency for storage. Storage costs alone ran about $1 billion annually during the early 1960's. In return, farmers agreed to limit the number of acres planted in supported crops. But price supports ignore a host of important farm products—most canning crops, poultry, eggs, and meat animals. Thus American agriculture polarizes into a structural dualism, composed, on the one hand, of those farms growing supported products, and, on the other, of farms producing outside the canopy of Federal price support. For our purposes, this segregation of farms in relation to government support will prove more useful than the more conventional division between large farms and small ones.

The Farmer and Technical Change

ALL U.S. farmers, both those who produce under government price supports and those who do not, are directly affected by the largely government inspired and financed revolution in agricultural technology. The dramatic metamorphosis in agricultural production is a result of technical breakthroughs in three areas—mechanical, chemical, and biological. The mechanical revolution, substituting inanimate energy for human and animal power, has increased the *per man* productivity of farm workers. The chemical revolution, less well-known to laymen, is equally important. The maturation of plants, and to some extent of animals, embodies a biochemical process. For plants, the key to growth is a favorable soil and climate combined with adequate moisture. When the climate is permissive, abundant moisture (through irrigation) and chemically correct soil (through the addition of fertilizers) often become a question of cost. Plants can be, and sometimes are, grown without the use of direct terrestial support; they need only a permissive atmosphere, sufficient moisture, and the requisite chemical inputs to flourish.

The revolution in agricultural biology has brought forth new strains of plants and animals, increasing yields and resisting nature's pestilency—bugs, other insects, disease and drought. The destruction of bug and insect life is now so widespread and so effective that conservationists warn us that we may face a "silent spring" as the lethal effects of pesticides spread through plant and animal phyla. Both the chemical and biological phases of the advance in agricultural science show their impact primarily on *per acre* productivity. When coupled with the labor-saving mechanical revolution, the chemical and biological discoveries have dramatically reduced the use of farm labor during a time of agricultural abundance.

In agriculture as in industry, technical progress and increases in labor productivity have made production steadily more capital intensive. Capital investment per agricultural worker was $21,300 in 1960 compared to an average of $15,900 in other industries.[13] And an increase in physical capital necessitates a rise in the complementary factor, human capital. On the larger farms the growing demand for technical skills is being met. The successful, large-scale farmer knows more about the intricacies of production detail than does the manager of any center firm. But in small-scale agriculture, both human and technical potential are underutilized. Even now the typical commercial farm should expand by a third or more to encompass available cost economies.

There was a time, stretching back no farther than the memory of many living men, when the small, isolated family farm was an efficient economic unit. Conveniently surrounded by pasture and field, the farm residence provided quick and easy access to the work place. Our rural grandfathers wasted little time in commuting. With primitive transportation facilities, bulky farm products—hay and feed grains—could best be reduced into a concentrated form for transport through the feeding of livestock.

In an earlier American era, cattle were forced to make their own passage to the nearest rail center. In those sections where high unit-value, nonfeed crops were cultivated, for example, Southern cotton and tobacco, the small family farm pattern was rejected in favor of plantation agriculture. The remoteness of early farmsteads elevated the cost and difficulty of securing necessary farm supplies, but these were few in number and small in quantity barely more than a generation ago. The ascendency of human and physical capital over land and water as agricultural prime movers is very recent.

Yet once agriculture becomes capital intensive, the remoteness of markets becomes a disabling fact. The most prosperous contemporary American agriculture is located near the outer rim of an urban complex. And the financial rewards in small-scale farming have flown away, lifted on the wings of technological change toward the suppliers of capital inputs and marketing technique.

The American farmer cannot, without the support of government, maintain a constant share of the income from agricultural production because his *contribution to output is progressively diminishing*. Perhaps an illustration will help underscore the farmer's dwindling role as a factor supplier. Since the 1930's, the number of horses and mules on American farms has declined by about 13 million, freeing no less than 46 million acres formerly devoted to growing feed. In 1920, about 90 million acres of valuable cropland were devoted to the feeding of horses and mules. By 1960, less than 10 million acres were so used. About one-fourth of all cropland in the U.S. was shifted in little more than a generation from animal subsistence to human consumption.[14] Farmers once received the returns from horse and mule multiplication, but they receive no part of the income from tractors and gasoline.

While seeing technical advance diminish his contribution as a factor supplier, the farmer has also witnessed a hostile development in marketing technology. Much of the advance in food processing and packaging has reduced spoilage and waste, losses occurring between the farm and the consumer. Improved

14. Hathaway, *op. cit.,* p. 99.

packaging, transportation, refrigeration, and product quality have sizably increased the yield of consumable farm output from a given harvest. Thus product-saving innovations have provided a perfect substitute for additional farm demand. Both the industrial supplier of agricultural inputs *and* the product-conserving agricultural distributor appropriate larger shares of the total agrobusiness income in very large part because they now contribute more to the finished, consumable product.

It is quite true, as farmers contend, that their industry is more competitive than those from which they buy and to which they sell. That the center firms surrounding farmers make, at times, a level of profits substantially above that going to purely competitive firms cannot be denied. Yet farmers are for the most part victims of an unusually rapid technology rather than of greedy monopolists. The technical transformation of agriculture has aided all Americans, including farmers, in numerous ways. It has removed the drudgery from farm work, reduced the uncertainties of production, created a greater variety of higher quality food, lowered food relative to nonfood prices, and supplied large quantities of produce for foreign distribution. But it has also left a large number of small farmers in the backwaters of American economic life. Indeed, average farm incomes have stagnated during years when technical efficiency advanced most rapidly.

The Federal government financially underpins the farming community and has done so since the early 1930's. But government has played a decidedly double hand in agricultural welfare. Since 1887, with the passage of the Hatch Act, the U.S. government in conjunction with the states has been the major source of finance for agricultural research and, equally important, the aggressive disseminator of advanced technical knowledge. A working division of labor has evolved between industry and government in agricultural research and development; the U.S. Department of Agriculture and the Federally subsidized state agricultural colleges have concentrated on basic research and the training of scientists, while private firms have undertaken a major portion of agricultural product development. In agricultural research and development, government and business have formed a potent partnership. Farmers seeking government aid are, in a sense, doing no more than asking for partial relief from the disruption ensuing from governmental activity in research.

Part of the technical advance stealing agricultural demand owes little or nothing to government support. The discovery of synthetic fibers, substitutes for cotton and wool, gives us a prime example. The government did not produce the agricultural revolution alone, and it has not extended the hand of price support to all agricultural products. But for those products the government does support through price maintenance, the Federal branch acts as a center economy, treating supported producers as satellites. Federal price support is to agriculture what administered pricing is to oligopolists and pattern bargaining is to center labor. The government brings stability, uniformity, and planning into agricultural markets just as these values, seldom considered by neoclassical theorists, are introduced into industrial markets by center economy management and labor.

Like center firms, the government presents its agricultural satellites with a stable market price. Unlike center firms, the government does not try to maximize satellite efficiency by offering a price that approximates minimum unit production costs. Thus government price support allows relatively inefficient agricultural producers to exist, while at the same time inveigling farm expansion where agricultural economies of scale can be used. Government encourages, but does not immediately force, agricultural efficiency. The largest producers receive the greatest payments from price supports, but all producers realize some benefit. And government satellites are, unlike those in the center syndrome, free of the phantom competition of potential industry entry by their major buyer.

Some Implications of Government-Agriculture Relations

IN BRIEF, for supported farmers, the Federal government provides many of the center economy's functions. These include a reasonably stable buying price, technical assistance, and financial aid in the form of loans and loan guarantees. As befits a democratic state, the support price is not pushed down near the purely competitive level and industry entry is not threatened. By allowing numerous small-scale, inefficient farmers to survive, support programs doubtlessly slow the growth by merger of large farms therein retarding the realization of scale economies. But many of these new scale economies are the offsprings of government-financed research and training. Since most of the labor-displacing technology was developed under government auspices, it is not unfitting that the government allow the rural dispossessed sufficient time to adjust to dramatic changes.

The exodus from farming has not been financially painful for those land-owning farmers deciding to sell. Agricultural land values have experienced considerable appreciation during the last generation, largely because the government's acreage allotment system made land a scarce agricultural factor. Despite low average agricultural earnings from 1950 to 1962, farm proprietors' equities, held mostly in rural real estate, climbed by $60 billion. This rise reflects a yearly growth of $5 billion during a time when net farm income averaged only $13 billion, and land appreciation is a tax-sheltered form of income. Farmers are the only Americans who can lose money year after year, then retire on their savings.[15] Farm workers who were forced out of agriculture, but who owned no land, have received no relief from this Federal cushion.

A number of American farms have the asset size and even the cash flow to qualify as center firms, but they all act like oversized periphery enterprises, forgoing diversification, integration, and regional dispersion in favor of an extreme cost consciousness. Why big farms act atavistically may stem from the homogeneous nature of agricultural products. It is probably no accident that the center firms in primary metals have also shown a tendency toward periphery patterns in spite of their enormous size.[16] In an affluent industrial economy, where weakly felt consumer wants are highly susceptible to advertising, inherently homogeneous products may suffer an enervating hiatus in mar-

15. Don Paarlberg, op. cit., p. 61. As David Ricardo and Henry George would have predicted, the benefits of government price supports have gone largely to landowners.
16. Alfred D. Chandler, Jr., comments on the lack of decentralization and diversification among metals firms in Strategy and Structure, M. I. T. Press, 1962, pp. 326–340.

keting. Both the farmer and the primary metal producer, separated from the consumer, enjoy only a derived demand.[17]

But the erosion of traditional markets by new, substitute materials is gradually moving firms in primary metals to end their self-imposed lethargy. Why has not the substitution of synthetics for cotton, packaging and storage for food production, stimulated our largest commercial farmers towards new endeavors? Difficult though it is to transfer the skills of agricultural management to other purposes, is it indeed impossible? A plausible answer seems to rest on farmers' lack of diversification incentive. By stockpiling surpluses the government cushioned the shock of technical change, muted the threat to agricultural survival. The government likewise stockpiled the outputs of nonferrous metal firms—aluminum, copper, lead, zinc—during the slack demand fifties. Even the large-scale suppliers of defense hardware have, in general, been reluctant to undertake significant diversification into nongovernment products.

One of the prime advantages of center firms, in addition to their financial strength, is their marketing organization and ability. A large portion of any consumer-oriented center firm's insurance against the future is its power to mold lingering favorable images, embracing both the firm and its products. But if, as in the case of agricultural products and primary metals, the output is inherently homogeneous, markets are not so easily influenced. Metals firms can, like Alcoa and Reynolds, buy into their markets (urban renewal) and begin selling to themselves; but the recourse to government as a buyer is inviting.

In the agricultural case, governmental intervention, while expensive, has produced socially useful results. While accumulating an invaluable storehouse of agricultural commodities for feeding the world's hungry millions, from friendly India to erstwhile cold warrior Russia, the government price support and acreage allotment program permitted the technically inspired growth of farm size to continue, slowed the out-migration

17. Alfred Marshall noted the affinity between homogeneous products and successful government intervention fifty years ago. "The industries in which Government Departments and Local Authorities have succeeded are few in number, but important. They are mainly concerned with 'things that sell themselves'; that is, things which are large in demand, and more or less standardized by natural causes." *Industry and Trade,* The Macmillan Company, 1919, p. 668.

of farm labor to a rate only slightly above the nonagricultural economy's labor absorption capacity, and stifled most agrarian unrest. In addition, supported agriculture has been set aside as a periphery preserve, an area where center economy firms have small incentive for entry.

Center-type organization has slowly invaded that segment of agriculture without government support. A common type of producer-buyer link in unsupported agriculture is contract growing, advance agreements between buyers and farmers predetermining the price paid for agricultural goods. Long used for canning and processing crops, contract production now dominates poultry and is spreading to meat animals. As a leading agricultural economist observes, "It is certainly more than coincidence that the most rapid development in risk-sharing contracts has been for farm products lacking price supports and having short-run price variations." [18]

Federal involvement in agriculture has enormously increased agricultural productivity. And the inelasticity of agricultural supply comprises one of the most significant potential developmental bottlenecks for a country striving to achieve full industrialization. Through the sustained creation and dissemination of technical knowledge, the U.S. government has removed one possible source of economic retardation.

Can it be an accident that government stockpiling of primary metals during the 1950's marks the beginning of a similar program in industries that threaten the formation of new growth and full-employment bottlenecks? And is it not likely that an American storehouse of primary metals, an input prerequisite for sustained industrial growth, might in time prove as useful to our underdeveloped friends as have our agricultural stocks?

The government has served the nonferrous metals industries primarily as a buyer and price stabilizer, not as a large-scale promoter of systematic technical change. Perhaps, in retrospect, we shall view the shortcoming of government's metal policy during the fifties as a one-sided pursuit of price support without the corollary emphasis on expanding nondefense metals research. The real failing of government policy toward homogeneous and

18. Hathaway, *op. cit.*, p. 153.

bottleneck commodities revolves around an inflexible allocation of technical talent and finance. For too long government has devoted an inordinate portion of our scarce technical resources to agriculture, which was yesterday's threatening growth strangler, and too little to basic metals, a full-employment bottleneck of today. But research is not the only element in the government's policy to foster growth and full employment. We must now turn to a consideration of the impact of government and the center economy on maintaining high levels of economic activity.

9. Government, the Center Economy, and Full Employment

SINCE THE DEPRESSION, the most debated of government's economic functions has been that of economic stabilizer. The Federal government is now generally recognized as the manager of aggregate demand, the guardian of national prosperity. Professional economic opinion has agreed, since at least the 1940's, that a major Federal responsibility is the provision of sufficient demand to provide full employment with a minimum of inflation. With the Employment Act of 1946, Congress and the President pledged themselves to this vital task. We have not, it is true, perfected as yet the means for fulfilling this worthy goal, but most Americans now accept its imminence. Since 1960, American presidents have shown a fundamental understanding of the principles involved in the stimulation of full employment as well as a willingness to undertake the necessary fiscal and monetary actions.

Macroeconomics in Brief

FULL EMPLOYMENT is a macroeconomic problem and the basic principles of macroeconomics are reasonably simple. We can do two things with our personal income—spend it or save it. If we save, we do not spend, and thus our income does not become income for someone else. Only money that is spent becomes income for others. This is a truism, because it merely examines the same transaction from two points of view. When I buy an object or service from someone, I make an expenditure but the seller receives income, and the two must equal one another. This point is fundamental to macroeconomics. Spending creates income, saving removes income from circulation.

This is clearly true of individuals, but it holds for other economic actors as well. Economic participants fall into four groups, three domestic and one foreign—individuals or households, business firms, government, and foreigners. The total spending of these four comprises the economy's aggregate, or total, demand. Consequently, aggregate demand is segmented into four types: spending by households (consumption expenditure), spending by business firms (investment expenditure), spending by government (government expenditure), and spending by foreigners (net foreign investment). The level of employment and output depend on the extent of aggregate demand. When the four types of expenditures are buoyant, unemployment is low and output is high.

Largely a function of income, consumption rises as total income expands and falls as it declines. Consumers tend to spend a constant amount of their incomes, saving less than 10 percent. The determinants of net foreign investment are many, but we need not consider them here for in the American economy their magnitude and domestic impact are relatively small. Thus the crucial determinants of the level of aggregate demand, output, and employment are investment expenditure and government expenditure.

The most volatile of the four expenditure types is investment. Businessmen invest because of profit expectations. If the demand for their output is low because of anemic total spending, their plants will be operating well below capacity. In a depression economy, new investment is typically limited to the replacement of worn-out equipment. Should national income, and thus consumption, begin to rise, the utilization of available plant capacity would increase, yielding more output and employing more labor. Once plant utilization reaches businessmen's desired levels, near the plant's productive capacity, businessmèn begin planning for additions to their productive facilities. Finally, if national income continues to rise, pushing many industries beyond desired levels of plant use, actual business investment in new plant and equipment takes a dramatic leap.

The strength of investment spending shows a direct, although lagged, relation to the extent of aggregate demand and its direction of movement. Beyond the point of desired plant utilization, investment spending takes an upward thrust, providing the final expenditure acceleration which propels the economy to full employment. The economic revival of the 1960's, for example, began in 1961. Investment remained weak during 1962 and 1963, while income and output continued to grow. But during 1964 and 1965, investment jumped into prominence, growing twice as fast as output. By January of 1966, investment accounted for 10½ percent of total demand, a postwar peak.

Government promotes the achievement of full employment in two basic ways. First, government expenditures buttress total spending, and taxation becomes an important means to possible government saving. In simple terms, prudent government fiscal policy, an indispensible macro tool, decrees that when aggregate demand is below the full employment level, government must spend more than it collects in taxes. When total spending threatens to exceed the amount necessary to full employment, creating inflationary pressures, the government should tax more than it spends. Government provides the expenditure flywheel, countering the excessive tendencies of investment both when it is lethargic and when it is hyperactive.

The second area of government initiative, monetary policy, operates on investment more directly. Much investment is made with borrowed money, making the rate of interest an important cost consideration. Even when investment funds are not borrowed, the going rate of interest shows an important "opportunity cost" to investors, for available funds can always be loaned rather than invested. Thus interest levels have a pronounced impact on the strength of investment expenditures, particularly when profit expectations are high. Monetary policy, then, involves manipulations of interest rates, and thus the availability of money, to foster a level of spending consistent with full employment.

The domination of key industries by center firms creates a potential pitfall to the government's macroeconomic objectives. The prevalence of oligopoly in key industries *allows* center firms to maintain and even increase prices on occasion before full employment is attained. In addition pattern bargaining by center unions may allow key industry labor to push wages well above levels justified by productivity gains, creating inflationary pressures prior to full employment. But the recently revitalized institution of "high level discussions of industry problems" between top officials in government, business, and labor proved so successful in the early sixties that the President's Council of Economic Advisors was able to report in 1966 that "private attitudes in key wage and price decisions are considerably more responsible." [1]

Notably, a prominent stumbling block to the government's sponsorship of satisfactory wage and price "responsibility" in critical industries came not from the oligopolistic center economy, but from the small-firm, decentralized union sectors like construction. Trying to reason with the 8,000 autonomous local unions bargaining with a multitude of regionalized construction firms led Secretary of Labor Willard Wirtz to lament the absence of center economy control in the building industry:

> Last year, it was steel, aluminum and maritime wages. The year before, it was automobiles. This year, it's construction. And construction is a very different matter from what we had to deal with in those other industries. In steel, for example, you talk with Abel [President of the Steelworkers] and you talk with Blough [Chairman, U.S. Steel Corporation] .There's no such center of gravity in the building trades.[2]

Secretary Wirtz speaks to a critical point. Government's macroeconomic function is to *control* the level of economic activity, boosting it when unemployment becomes excessive and slowing

1. *Economic Report of the President,* U.S. Government Printing Office, January, 1966, p. 63.
2. *Forbes,* Vol. 97, No. 7 (April 1, 1966), p. 17.

it down when inflation threatens. And the center economy, with its visible seats of economic power, is an invaluable, perhaps indispensable, organization structure through which the economy's pivotal sectors can be influenced. In short, once government thoroughly accepts the full implications of maintaining maximum output and employment, center control of critical sectors becomes an aid to government policy, periphery domination becomes a hindrance.

The Regulation of Business

IF THE center economy is a cohort of government in the search for full employment, what does this imply for antitrust? Is the government attempting with its left hand to strike down that which its right hand finds indispensable? Competition among the few has macroeconomic advantages not taken into account by traditional microeconomics. Yet production by a single firm, or a very few firms acting as one, may destroy all forms of competition, that between marketing departments *and* between research departments. Most economists are willing to forgo the theoretical advantages of perfect competition, but few, if any, want to see oligopoly replaced with perfect monopoly. Thus the Justice Department's antitrust division must continue to punish restraints of trade as evidenced by price fixing, obvious restrictions of production, market allocation, and the flagrant suppression of innovation. The danger of antitrust, however, lies in a national policy giving preference to firms of a particular size, administrative structure, product mix, or geographic spread. Center firms, particularly those rooted in key industries, are usually oligopolistic. And as oligopolists, they are the beneficiaries of pure profits (profits above those they would receive under a purely competitive market structure). Yet it is not, as traditional neo-classical economics suggests, pure profits in themselves that are socially undesirable. The harm from pure profits comes when they are put to socially undesirable ends.

Perhaps a brief consideration of two noted candidates for the asocial label will help illustrate this point. Exorbitant executive salaries and advertising are outstanding. One sometimes hears complaints about the extravagant compensations paid center firm managers. In a highly developed industrial country like the United States, nonhuman productive factors ᵣ̣re relatively abundant. But creative management is always in sho᷃ supply. Since managers fashion the system they manage, they are subject to a crude Say's law: their supply creates its own demand. As suppliers of a perpetually scarce factor, they command, not surprisingly, an abundant financial reward.

The line between a necessary return to a vital and scarce factor, center firm management, and excessive executive incomes based on monopoly pricing power is difficult to draw. Yet prominent cases of managerial excess stand out. In 1962, when automobile sales had yet to reach record levels, the salaries and bonuses paid the fifty-six officers and directors of General Motors exceeded the combined remuneration received by the President of the United States, the Vice-President, 100 U.S. Senators, 435 members of the U.S. House of Representatives, the nine Supreme Court justices, the ten cabinet members, and the governors of the fifty states.[3]

Advertising is a second use of pure profits largely condemned by economists. The case against advertising can be summarized as follows: the object of a private enterprise economy is to provide the greatest satisfaction to society; consumers are the best judges of their own satisfactions, and in the aggregate they compose society. Any resources not directly allocated by consumers will not, except through improbable accident, maximize consumer satisfaction; resources devoted to advertising are allocated by advertisers, not consumers; hence resources spent on advertising are less than optimally efficient. In addition, economic theory conventionally assumes that consumer wants are autonomous. If producers create, through advertising, the wants they serve, are we not caught in a squirrel cage of economic activity, producing to create employment rather than to satisfy genuine human desires?[4] Surely the American economy rests on a more secure utilitarian base than this.

3. A. H. Raskin, "Walter Reuther's Great Big Union," in Richard A. Lester (ed.), *Labor: Readings on Major Issues*, Random House, Inc., 1965, p. 99.
4. In *The Affluent Society, op. cit.*, John Kenneth Galbraith contends that American production *is* largely for the purpose of providing employment.

Some advertising, like some level of executive compensation, does indeed serve a valid social purpose. When used to inform consumers of the quality, price, and availability of specific products, customers receive useful information. But much contemporary corporate advertising belongs in the public relations category of "image forming," stressing the firm as much as the product, pleasant daydreams rather than real product characteristics. These ads must be justified largely as entertainments, a service where the orthodox emphasis on consumer choice is perfectly valid. Are we not capable of choosing our own entertainments, allocating our expenditures to those enjoyments yielding the highest satisfaction per dollar spent?

Executive salaries exceeding the opportunity cost of their recipient's employment outside an oligopolistic firm may involve trivial amounts of the nation's income, but advertising does not. The yearly cost of advertisement exceeds $14 billion. Yet pure profits also go for socially desirable purposes. That part of pure profits retained by the firm after dividends have been paid is the firm's discretionary income. Especially during periods of prosperity much of it is spent for investment in new plant capacity, particularly in industries where technical change is rapid. And new investment is the touchstone of economic growth.

Many center firms also engage in privately financed research and development. While much of this effort is devoted to defensive research, paralleling work done in other firms, most research and development work undoubtedly confers some ultimate benefits on consumers. The least useful research is that linked to making minor product differentiations, useful in the firm's advertising campaigns, but containing little real merit for consumers. The drug and automobile industries are noted for such abuses. Still the marketing of new products and improvements in the quality of the old lie in the American tradition, expanding the range of at least petty consumer choice.

For antitrusters, the critical question emerges. How can the abuses of center-economy abundance be checked without curbing the social uses of center-firm largesse? One obvious method is to tax the undesirable expenditures of center-firm profits. Such a tax raises several problems of definition: for instance, what level of executive compensation, and what type of advertising, is without social justification? The burden of our argument, however, is this. The center economy exists, and its existence is in many ways socially useful. Economists should maintain an attitude of institutional laissez-faire, recommending policies that curb socially undesirable activities while promoting desirable ones, no matter what their institutional origin.

Perpetual Prosperity: Full Employment Maintained

As WE HAVE SEEN, a high level of investment spending is essential to achieve full employment. Yet once full employment arrives, a policy dilemma appears. While income generated by investment spending is necessary to the creation of full employment, investment's increment to productive capacity makes the maintenance of full employment difficult. The precise level of investment just sufficient to maintain, but not exceed, full employment provides a narrow range of policy tolerance. If, once full employment is extant, businessmen try to keep earlier rates of investment spending, a rate twice as rapid as the expansion of output, they will merely succeed in driving up prices. Labor and critical materials, full-employment bottlenecks, prevent the realization of investment rates prevailing just prior to full employment. Unless investors reduce their investment plans, they will bid up the price of industrial inputs as they scramble for newly scarce supplies.

If, on the other hand, businessmen suddenly find their present plant capacity adequate to today's demands and those anticipated for the immediate future, investment spending may fall as dramatically as it once increased, lowering the economy below full employment unless the government fills the expenditure gap with increments in government outlays or prompt tax cuts. In short, once full employment is reached, investment cannot grow at its former rate; any attempt to do so feeds inflation. Yet investment must not fall to recession levels, since a too severe drop fosters unemployment.

The solution to full employment's perpetuation is difficult, but in broad outline the implications for government are clear.

Monetary and fiscal policies designed to stimulate investment and thus *create* full employment are not sufficient to *sustain* high employment indefinitely. The requisite for maintaining full employment without inflation, of achieving perpetual prosperity, is a dynamic equilibrium between *industry capacity* and *industry demand,* particularly in the acutely sensitive key industries. Demand and the productive capacity for its fulfillment must grow up together in a dynamic equilibrium if full employment is to be maintained without inflation. Demand must not be allowed to fall much below capacity, tempting investment to recede hurriedly, or pushed much above capacity, creating irresistible inflationary pressures.

At least in theory, it is possible for this dynamic equilibrium to be continued by government's manipulation of aggregate demand alone, leaving decisions about new industrial capacity solely in private hands. But that government is twice armed in its pursuit of perpetual prosperity which can exert some influence over *both* aggregate demand and capacity creation. Businessmen's profit expectations are notoriously subject to cumulative causation, overly optimistic during prosperity, and despairing during economic downturns. Variations in the money supply and adjustments in interest rates, when performed with subtle timing and sufficient force, may effectively restrain over-investment at full employment; but no monetary policy has proved equal to the task of lifting investment when deflated profit expectations are omnipresent.

The motivational underpinnings of investment spending, businessmen's profit expectations, are psychological wisps. The least coercive, and therefore the most politically acceptable, form of government influence over investors centers on discrete manipulations of the climate of investment opinion. And indeed the persuasion of center businessmen by admonition and harassment marked the first half of the 1960's. When specific investment climates must be adjusted, industry structure is very important. Key industries dominated by a few center firms set an uniquely favorable arena for government persuasion. The Department of Commerce is currently experimenting with an econometric model of the U.S. which may, in time, lead to a scientific judgment of perpetual prosperity's prerequisites.[5] Even now, when economic programming is still in its infancy, perfect computation presents a more appealing ideal than does a return to perfect competition. Most large firms, solicitous of their public image and wary of government's buying and antitrust powers, are responsive to government's suggestions when tactfully proferred. Although joint exercises in economic rationality have not yet been applied with much vigor to domestic investment, conferences between center management, center labor, and high government officials have already borne fruit in other areas.

Sweet reasonableness and the public interest may persuade center managers and labor leaders to hold in abeyance their price- and wage-setting powers before full employment is reached, but such persuasions cannot dim the real pressures on prices and wages at full employment. A fundamental difficulty inherent in maintaining a full employment economy through time relates to an economy's technical structure. The elasticity of supply of industrial inputs varies. At full employment, or just before full employment is reached, producers begin to encounter shortages of skilled labor and primary metals, significantly nonferrous metals. While Presidential admonition toward labor and management, concentrating on the metal industries (aluminum, copper, steel), may halt the use of monopoly wage and price power before full employment, persuasion alone falters after full employment arrives, bringing with it a demand for bottleneck inputs exceeding their short-run supply.

Should government have the luck or foresight to stockpile critical metals, as did the U.S. during the slack fifties, short-run pressures on demand can be alleviated by reducing the government hoard. The output of foreign producers can also be utilized if foreigners have excess capacity in primary metals. Yet both stockpiles and foreign sources of these metals supply only temporary relief; and skilled labor cannot be stockpiled. In summary, it is *input* bottlenecks, beginning with skilled labor and primary metals, that create irresistible pressures on wages and prices,

5. The latest developments in macroeconomic mathematical experimentation by government are reported in Maurice Liebenberg, Albert A. Hirsch, and Joel Popkin, "A Quarterly Econometric Model of the United States: A Progress Report," *Survey of Current Business*, Vol. 46, No. 5 (May, 1966).

eventually threatening the preservation of prosperity, even while aggregate demand remains high.

The creation of an economy capable of sustaining full employment requires that the government maintain a full-employment level of aggregate demand, discourage the use of monopoly power by business and labor, *and* break a series of specific factor bottlenecks.

Economists conventionally discuss full employment in terms of aggregate demand and aggregate supply. When confining one's attention to the achievement of full employment, aggregate analysis is sufficient. But full employment is an analytical watershed. Before full employment the U.S. economy experiences few input shortages; when full employment is reached, the analytical emphasis must shift if the economy is to *maintain* maximum output and employment. A continuation of full employment necessitates a disaggregated, structural analysis, pinpointing the full-employment level of demand and supply for specific bottleneck industries. There is, for example, some level of steel production, given the current mix of aggregate demand at full employment and the production functions of American firms, that is consistent with perpetuating prosperity. The full-employment level of steel demand will vary through time, but steel capacity must be kept adequate to assure the maintenance of full employment without inflation.

Further still, no economy can hold perpetual prosperity without an adequate supply of human capital. One responsibility of government is the provision of enough capacity in the education industry to prevent the inelasticity of skilled and professional labor from becoming the first cause of an inflation that ultimately pulls the economy below full employment. Recent steps by government in this vital area include the "G. I. Bills" and the training provisions in the "war on poverty." In fact, the war on poverty aids prosperity in two ways. As the poor are brought into the mass-consuming middle class, domestic demand rises, offsetting habits of oversaving in an affluent society. And the training provisions of the poverty war help to relieve the skilled labor bottleneck caused partly by the trainees' rise from poverty.

Our thesis, then, in a few words. An economy of perpetual full employment requires more of government than wise monetary and fiscal policy. Perpetual abundance insists on a coordination of investment with demand in bottleneck sectors. This dynamic equilibrium in selected industries can more easily be established when major decisions become the responsibility of a few visible decision makers. The center economy presents a fortuitous industry structure for the attainment of the macro goals of full employment and economic growth accompanying it. The U.S. economic system stands poised between the laissez-faire, fragmented industrial economy of the past where lapses from full employment are inevitable, and a centrally planned economy where business cycles, as we know them, are impossible.[6] The pattern of center-economy—key-industry convergence provides the organizational means for avoiding the familiar unemployment hardships of the past while alleviating the unfortunate consequences of rigid central planning. The Federal government makes perpetual prosperity more difficult to achieve when it disrupts the center economy. Government must, rather, set rules of business conduct which nudge center firms toward the social good.

Government and the Long Run

THE center economy aids growth and prosperity and, in reciprocity, the continuation of full employment is good for the center economy. Superior size, with creative management and substantial financial resources, gives center firms an astronautic perspective on economic choice. By expanding the financial discretion of the center, full employment propels center firms' growth and sharpens their maneuverability. It is no accident that American merger movements were strong during the prosperous 1920's and 1960's. Center firms can use their incremented monetary reserves and stock values to diversify, and they can engage in additional research and development, reinforcing their technical lead over loyal opposition rivals. Some center-firm gains flow into new in-

---

6. For a short but informative discussion of the economic prerequisites for business fluctuations, see Howard J. Sherman, *Elementary Aggregate Economics,* Appleton-Century-Crofts, 1966, pp. 24–27.

vestments, contributing more productive and efficient capital equipment. And supplements to already large advertising budgets tend to strengthen consumer preferences for center products.

Should the American government succeed in creating perpetual prosperity, the U.S. economy will take on a new industrial structure. Much of the present industrial pattern is the outgrowth of an economic system subjecting business enterprises to periodic retrenchment. When businessmen overinvest, the next recession saddles them with burdensome excess capacity. If they expand into new fields too quickly, an abrupt decline in aggregate demand may encumber the new venture with large losses before it is integrated into the firm's organizational apparatus. In short, the American experience with recurrent fluctuations in economic activity has cast over business an air of caution.

This underlying conservatism, painfully learned from past recessions, restrains all business firms, large and small. But it is most significant to center firms, for it is they who possess the greatest economic potential. Should perpetual prosperity negate the center's self-restraint, new confidence will enhance their lead. When all firms are restrained, it is the weak who suffer least, having less economic potency to reign in. It is not unlikely that the qualitative differences between center and periphery have remained largely hidden from professional economists until now because of the checks that economic fluctuations imposed on center potential.

When demand taxes the economy, as it does during wartime, it becomes quite clear that America's productive power lies in the center economy. In wars, economic growth becomes the economy's overriding goal. And so must growth play the central part in an economy determined to create perpetual prosperity without war.

The motives of men are said to be complex, ambivalent, and submerged, yet perhaps the dramatic return of business confidence and the amazing strength of business investment during the middle 1960's sprang in no small measure from the unspoken intuitions of businessmen, particularly those in center firms, who perceived that perpetual prosperity is now a technical possibility. [PHILIP O. GEIER, JR., President, Cincinnati Milling Machine Company — *We may have pauses, but I don't think they'll be as rough as the downturn we had in 1958.*][7] Should it arrive, it will be accompanied by an unleashing of center economy potential that will startle men everywhere, and not least those whose contact with American business is most intimate.

The Future of the American Economy

THE FUTURE can never be seen with precision, yet a few indistinct shapes now outline an economy yet unborn. We have seen that the U.S. government seems genuinely committed to the creation of full employment, and the fiscal and monetary mechanisms for its achievement are well established. There is still much work to be done on macroeconomic techniques, but the remaining tasks are in the nature of marginal adjustments in known devices. The U.S. economy is fully capable of full employment; the voting public seems indisposed to settle for less.

And full employment, driving into the future, transforms the economy into one of perpetual prosperity. We know little about this still uncharted terrain, save that a rough coordination between capacity and demand, particularly in critical key industries, seems essential. A mature, industrial economy operates under what engineers would consider very broad tolerances. Underinvestment or overpricing in, for example, steel, is unlikely to prove fatal in any one year. But even the wealthiest of nations does not have unlimited economic latitude, and ultimately the government must assure that full employment is not threatened by human caprice at the industrial heart.

Our point briefly stated is this. Since Marshall, microtheory has depended on an economic structure dominated by the actions of consumers and business firms. The only major innovation in Marshallian analysis during the twentieth century has been the introduction of oligopoly theory and the analysis of monopolistic competition. Macroeconomics, born in the depression, introduced a third economic actor, government. The success of government in achieving high employment, and of firms in satisfying consumers' strongly felt wants, has *both* created a new economic structure *and* elevated a new type of economic problem to the forefront. To *maintain* full employment, the economy must grow

7. *Forbes*, Vol. 98, No. 11 (December 1, 1966), p. 30.

rapidly. And the key to rapid growth in a fully employed economy is the long-run factor of technology.

When the economy *achieves* the purpose for which Keynes wrote, when the creation of full employment is no longer our overriding concern, we are free once again to concentrate on the classical goals of long-run progress. But in the long run, we cannot assume the structure of institutions as given. We cannot know what shape government, corporations, and consumer demand will take in the future, but we can be certain that they will not have their present form. The beauty of short-run analysis, the source of its analytical precision and rigor, lies in the assumption that long-run factors—the institutional structure, population, technology—remain substantially constant. But these long-run subjects undergo cumulative change. Institutional structures and technology not only refuse to remain constant, but are now changing at an increasingly rapid pace. How, then, can economists hope to formulate satisfactory theories of the long run that are more than sheer speculation? Is not an unknown long-run future anyone's guess?

While the mathematical precision of contemporary macro- and microanalysis may be confined for all time to the short run, economists do not face the long run completely unarmed. We know, for instance, that the propelling force in long-run growth is technological change. And this change must be embodied in specific techniques organized by economic institutions. Thus the critical motive emblem of long-run growth is the structure of economic institutions. Business firms, government, nonprofit organizations must, on the whole, stimulate technical progress and implement it. Unlike macroanalysis, an economic theory formed around technological progress need not center on the organizational cleavage between government and industry. Research, development, and innovation are the prime concerns, and both the public and private sectors must have a role in their promotion.

We discovered earlier that the center economy is already sensitive to the pull of technology. Where technology leads the center must ultimately follow, for only by so doing can it preserve itself from the quicksand of change. An emerging pattern of corporate organization for technically progressive center firms places a central research department, staff management, and a central source of funds at the corporate heart. Operating divisions are loosely tied to this nucleus. The pivotal research and development staff creates new products, explores the market potential of new technology, and supplies new divisions, created to market research discoveries, with technical personnel. Such new divisions usually have considerable antonomy. Firms approximating this model include Minnesota Mining and Manufacturing, Carborundum, AMF, Brunswick, and Union Carbide.[8] Technical mobility, the key to organizational survival, is built into the firm's structure. The normal institutional resistance to change is effectively circumvented. One private entity, the Bell Labs (a division of the Bell Telephone System) has served as a central research organization for a number of electronics firms, offering nonexclusive licenses for semiconductors developed by Bell in addition to giving technical advice.

When center corporations are attuned to a dynamic technological climate, the evolution of center firms can be powerfully influenced by a government that directs technology. The steering wheel of the technological vehicle is the allocation of pivotal technical inputs—research funds and scientific talent. A government-financed laboratory, operating in the mode of the private Bell Labs, might effectively provide technological stimulus and new business opportunities for other American firms. Government development work might be concentrated in those areas showing, for example, (1) sharply rising costs at full employment, (2) significant price upturns at full employment, and/or (3) long delivery dates at full employment.[9]

In the past, the Federal government has underwritten technical change primarily in response to an immediate crisis—to wage war and to pacify farmers. The bulk of publicly financed research and development now goes for national survival. Can it not be as effective in securing the general welfare? Government-directed

---

8. U.S. Senate, Select Committee on Small Business, *The Role and Effect of Technology in the Nation's Economy*, Part V, 88th Congress, 1st Session, 1964, p. 648.

9. Alfred Marshall endorsed government research in key industries a half century ago, but warned against the influence of businessmen with vested interests. *"The National Physical Laboratory and the Committee of the Privy Council on Scientific and Industrial Research are recognized as doing work of the highest value. But there is danger that, when relying on private advice, a department or the cabinet may be influenced by biased opinion in deciding what industries should be aided on account of their exceptional importance as "key" or "pivotal" industries. And yet the State has clearly some duties in this matter; especially when supporting independent organized effort."* Industry and Trade, The Macmillian Company, 1919, p. 671.

research is not a radical or an unique idea; indeed, it is a most conservative one. The Federal government already finances about two-thirds of all U.S. research and development efforts, employing a large segment of America's scientific talent. What we are suggesting is primarily a shift in the emphasis of research from defense and agriculture to other industries. Should peace break out we will have a large cadre of scientific talent available for reassignment, and even now we are, perhaps, paying too great a price for military science. As the history of agriculture and defense vividly show, high-priority, government-sponsored research transforms industries. We must not allow even marginal quantities of such tremendous power to escape into areas boasting less than the highest social merit.

The United States' economy now stands on the threshold of perpetual prosperity. When, in the next several years or decades, that threshold is passed, the center economy will constitute a basic support. The constancy of long-run center costs is an essential ingredient of a free-enterprise economy enjoying continuous full employment without disruptive inflation. For too long economists have visualized center firms as simply multiple oligopolists, condemned to academic censure by the downward slope of their revenue curves.

Yet when short-run problems cease to occupy our full energies, when a mature, industrialized economy finally grasps the implications of economic abundance, the science of economics will once again be free to resume its standing as a moral science. The new long-run economics, focusing on technology and the evolution of economic organization, will be able to set aside the dated public-private, competition-monopoly, socialist-capitalist debates in order to concentrate on expanding the possibilities of human awareness and achievement. We are not, alas, quite done with the short run. The child must learn to walk before it can run. We now toddle sufficiently well to begin exploring the next stage. Having learned how to employ ourselves, we must begin to ponder questions of greater duration. How, in our time, will we advance the expansion of human capabilities? We are leaving a maturing economy, but is its structure best-suited to man's inner unity and maturation?

10. A Summing Up

ALTHOUGH MOST OF the previous chapters contain speculations on the implications of dualism for economic policy, a summary of these suggestions and the arguments supporting them may prove useful. What follows is a brief synopsis of our conclusions. We consider first the traditional microeconomic goals of consumer resource allocation and economic efficiency, then the macroeconomic objective of full employment with tolerable price stability, and finally the long-run goal of full-employment growth.

Microeconomic Goals: Consumer Allocation of Resources and Efficiency

MICROTHEORY tells us that monopoly retards efficiency. If the American economy were perfectly competitive, and if the factors of production were perfectly mobile, capital and labor would leave poor employments for more promising ones until in time a dollar of investment or an hour of work earned the same remuneration regardless of where it was employed. When all productive factors are earning an income equal to their most remunerative alternative employment in a perfectly competitive economy, nothing can be gained by shifting resources between industries.

To the extent that product and factor markets are less than

perfect, microtheory informs us that the total economy's efficiency declines. We may be producing too few automobiles in the oligopolistic automobile industry (is this possible?) and too many shoes in the more competitive shoe industry. If all firms producing automobiles, shoes, and other goods were small enough to be price takers, so that prices allowed no monopoly profit, consumers might well choose more cars. If we ignore plant economies of scale (those resulting from large plants rather than large firms), the theory is, at least in principle, correct. But numerous studies of the gains we should expect from the elimination of monopoly all reach the same conclusion. The efficiency cost of monopoly is trivial; it can probably be overcome by a single month's economic growth.[1] If the center economy and its attached unions perpetuate monopoly, the best evidence suggests that the problem is not at present a major one.

Still production can be inefficient even when factors receive no more than their opportunity cost. Other indicators of excessive production costs include excess plant capacity, manipulative advertising (as opposed to advertising that provides useful information), and plants too small to utilize technical scale economies. The first measure is of theoretical interest only. It is virtually impossible to distinguish excess capacity resulting from monopoly from that caused by falling or fluctuating demand. Here economists can do little more than speculate. And part of the total expenditure on advertising helps support services of the mass media (television, radio, newspapers) that consumers would no doubt finance in another way if advertising did not exist. Another part provides useful information about the characteristics of goods and services and their availability. When these two sources of socially beneficial advertising outlay are subtracted, the cost of "manipulative advertising" would probably not exceed 1 percent of the national income.[2]

Finally, the most extensive study of scale economies in American industry concludes that most output in the fifteen industries

---

1. The empirical evidence of this point is summarized in Harvey Leibenstein, "Allocative Efficiency vs. 'X-Efficiency'," *American Economic Review*, Vol. LVI, No. 3 (June, 1966), pp. 392–397. Professor Leonard Weiss estimates that monopoly profits in the U.S. economy total no more than 2 to 4 percent of the national income. See Weiss, *Case Studies in American Industry*, John Wiley & Sons, Inc., 1967, p. 318.

2. Weiss, *op. cit.*, p. 327, suggests the 1 percent figure.

included came from plants of efficient size.[3] A more recent investigation by the same economist found that Britain, France, Italy, Japan, India, Sweden, and Canada all had plants of less efficient size than did the United States.[4] Since large plants tend to be associated with large firms, the center economy may deserve some credit on this point, although the large size of the U.S. economy is probably the most important factor. In industries where mass or process production is technically feasible, small firms may be *forced* to rely on the more expensive batch production. The machine tool industry may be an example of an American industry where mass production has been retarded by a radically fluctuating demand as well as the predominance of small enterprises.

Macroeconomic Goals: Full Employment with Price Stability

UNLIKE MONOPOLY, the economic cost of unemployment is far from trivial. By one authoritative estimate, a 1 percent increase in employment yields a 3 percent increase in output.[5] The failure to maintain full employment can easily cost the American consumer more than all other possible inefficiencies combined. During the postwar period the U.S. economy's greatest inefficiency *has* been its failure to provide full employment. Virtually all professional economic opinion attributes this costly failure to poor Federal government policy. Few economists doubt that government can, using prudent monetary and fiscal policy, create full employment.

Government's ability to provide both full employment and price stability is much more controversial. During the 1950's several economists found evidence of "administered inflation," a tendency for firms and unions in the center economy to increase prices even during periods of unemployment and excess capacity. No economist denies that inflationary pressures intensify when full employment is reached. Although some center firms and

3. Joe S. Bain, *Barriers to New Competition,* Harvard University Press, 1956.
4. Bain, *International Differences in Industry Structure,* Yale University Press, 1966.
5. Arthur M. Okun, "The Gap Between Actual and Potential Output," in A. M. Okun (ed.), *The Battle against Unemployment,* W. W. Norton & Company, Inc., 1965, pp. 13–22.

unions undoubtedly took advantage of their monopolistic pricing power in the 1950's, after 1959 prices in concentrated industries rose no more than those in unconcentrated sectors.[6] And the relative price stability accompanying the rapid expansion of the early 1960's suggests that "inflation permissive" government policy may have been an important factor during the earlier inflation. Clearly government *can* make noninflationary price and wage guidelines effective while the economy is not fully employed if it has the political will.

Perpetual Prosperity: Full-Employment Growth

ALTHOUGH THE "administered inflation" explanation of general price rises during the 1950's remains controversial, a number of center firms, particularly those in primary metals, did raise prices while supporting considerable excess capacity. Perhaps strong government pronouncements reinforcing wage and price guidelines would have tempered the tendency to exploit the opportunities of concentration. But voluntary guidelines are unlikely to provide a sufficient detriment to industrial price increases at full employment when excess capacity disappears. The creation of full employment by government policy may encounter political barriers, and these may prove disabling to a prudent policy because of the necessity for precise policy timing. The decision to raise or lower taxes, for example, may be delayed in Congress until the action originally recommended is no longer appropriate. But the *maintenance* of full employment, once it is achieved, encounters severe technical bottlenecks.

Consider, for example, an increased demand for output during prosperity that calls forth a high level of investment expenditure. Near full employment, the demand for capital goods, and particularly the primary metal inputs to capital goods, begins to exceed their plant capacity, inducing a rapid rise in capital goods prices. The cost of investment goes up. A careful study of price data from consumer goods, producer goods, and raw materials for a number of years just prior to 1938 showed that during prosperity consumer goods prices rose by 12 percent, producers goods by

6. Weiss, *op. cit.*, p. 330.

21 percent, and raw materials by 23 percent.[7] A more recent study indicates that except during World War II, the *relative* price of investment goods rose between 1929 and 1959.[8] While construction prices (an industry not dominated by center firms) continued to increase faster than the general price level after 1959, producers durable-equipment prices increased much less rapidly than the general price level during the early 1960's. Until the 1960's, investors in consumer goods industries found that their expansion plans were frustrated at full-employment by an investment-cost—output-price squeeze. And their declining investment often signaled the onset of the next recession. Undoubtedly the wage-price guidelines of the 1960's must receive much of the applause for having reversed this well-established pattern.

A peacetime increase in aggregate demand stimulates the market for primary metals more rapidly than that of any other productive sector.[9] When the suppliers of primary metals (steel, aluminum, copper, zinc) approach plant capacity, they begin to post price increases. And plant capacity is reached in these industries before labor is fully employed.[10] Government's macroeconomic policies are at present largely confined to the maintenance of aggregate demand and the promulgation of voluntary wage and price guidelines. When successful, these are sufficient to create full employment without industrial inflation, but they are not capable of *maintaining* noninflationary full employment. Center firms supplying primary metals and producers durables may try to increase prices before their output reaches plant capacity; but before economic capacity is reached, cost per unit is still falling. Any attempt to raise prices when costs are falling

7. Frederick C. Mills, *Price-Quantity Interactions in Business Cycles,* National Bureau of Economic Research, 1946.
8. Bert G. Hickman, *Investment Demand in the Sixties,* Brookings Institution, 1966, pp. 103–104; also R. A. Gordon, "Price Changes: Consumers' and Capital Goods," *American Economic Review,* Vol. LI, No. 5 (December, 1961), pp. 937–957.
9. Bert G. Hickman, *Investment Demand and U.S. Economic Growth,* Brookings Institution, 1965, pp. 184–185.
10. In December, 1965, the nonferrous metals industries were operating at 103 percent of capacity. They were the only industry group operating above 100 percent capacity. See *Economic Report of the President,* U.S. Government Printing Office, 1966, p. 68. (Although capacity is an exceedingly difficult concept to define, in general it refers to the maximum output for which plant facilities were designed. It is usually possible to exceed this figure by increasing production costs, thus allowing output to exceed 100 percent of "capacity.")

is a clear indication of administered pricing, the use of monopoly power. Government wage-and-price guidelines, strongly encouraged by an informed and determined President, can usually prevent increases of this nature.

But once plant capacity is reached and exceeded, short-run costs inevitably rise. When this happens, no degree of moral suasion can maintain price constancy. And when the prices of primary metals and producers goods begin to rise, boosting the cost of investment more rapidly than the rise in investment's expected return in the consumer goods sector, continued full employment is endangered. When full employment is achieved, the demand for goods rises less rapidly than during the approach to full employment. Yet the cost of investment tends to rise. Eventually the rate of investment growth falls, followed soon by a decline in the absolute level of investment. A new recession is underway.

Viewed from this perspective, a major problem of maintaining full employment is one of breaking full-employment supply bottlenecks. This is true even with firm Federal guidelines. The two most important bottlenecks, as we saw in Chapter 3, are skilled labor and primary metals. Private firms provide much on-the-job training in industrial skills, but they do not provide enough trained personnel soon enough to prevent a debilitating skilled labor shortage at full employment. Government must ensure the availability of a supplementary skilled labor supply. The primary metals form another full-employment supply bottleneck. This impediment to continued prosperity can be eliminated by the adoption of a government metals program similar to the basic agriculture commodity program.

Primary metals are highly susceptible to process production. And process production dramatically lowers costs *if* producers can operate continuous flow plants at near capacity levels. Yet the primary metals are peculiarly subject to wide fluctuations in demand as economic activity rises and falls. Thus most primary metals produced by U.S. firms are still manufactured using batch techniques, for batch production minimizes the high cost of excess capacity during periods of slack demand. The assurance of a continuous level of high demand, with government·

purchases supplementing private demand when necessary, would allow metals producers to move vast portions of their capacity into lower-cost process plants, while permitting government to stabilize metals prices during full-employment peaks by selling off a portion of its metals stockpile. Should the government's metals holdings grow during some period at an unanticipated rate, the surplus might well be transferred to selected under-developed nations as foreign aid in the manner now used for distributing U.S. food surpluses. A program of metals productivity research financed with government funds might also be beneficial if productivity gains in the industry prove unsatisfactory.

In short, to encourage perpetual prosperity, the government should act as an economic center to the primary metals industry. Yet full-employment growth demands much more than the institutionalizing of the *ad hoc* metals program begun in the 1950's under the banner of stockpiling "strategic materials" for defense. The most critical factor in full-employment growth is technical progress. Here consumer choice, the basic allocation standard of microtheory, is conspicuously ineffectual. How much technical progress do consumers want? How can they reveal their preference for any specific rate in the private economy? Rapid technical change can be socially disruptive to those who are experiencing it, as the forced migration from American agriculture would have been without government intervention. Yet technical improvement is necessary to sustained growth at full employment.

Center firms are capable of providing part of the technical impetus. They are a major source of minor or improvement innovations, but only a minor sponsor of major radical innovations. Large corporate laboratories produced nylon, the transistor, Freon refrigerants, tetraethyl lead, and Krilium, but these are exceptions to the center firms' tendency to stress relatively minor product improvements in research. Of course, a host of minor improvements may have a large impact on productivity and living standards.[11]

11. Daniel Hamberg, *R & D: Essays on the Economics of Research and Development,* Random House, Inc., 1966, pp. 35–44, summarizes the evidence on the contribution of large and small firms to research and development. See also Edwin Mansfield, *The Economics of Technological Change,* W. W. Norton & Company, Inc., 1968.

Major innovations are one distinguishing mark of the pioneering loyal opposition, such as Polaroid, the Control Data Corporation, and National Steel. Yet basic research, while socially useful, is not likely to be very profitable for many private firms, large or small. Neither jet aircraft nor atomic energy were financed during the development stage by private enterprises, although both are now used in the private sector. Business firms are significantly limited to underwriting technical changes that promise relatively short-run profit within the existing economy. Center firms will do this research and development job reasonably well, particularly when stimulated by foreign competition, pioneering loyal opposition competitors, or a research threat to their established markets by other center enterprises. But private firms cannot be expected to finance and promote the bulk of research efforts intended to change the nature of existing industries and thus make a host of expensive capacity obsolete. Research of this kind must originate in the main with government financing. In addition, government may find it useful to provide low-interest loans for new or existing firms interested in turning government-sponsored inventions into innovations. [JOHN R. MOORE, Executive Vice President, North American Aviation — *We have a hugh stockpile of technology just spoiling on the shelves.*] [12]

Several economists have studied and debated the research and development contributions of small, medium-sized, and large firms during recent years. Their collective findings indicate that smaller firms, and even individuals, still contribute more inventions and innovations than one would expect, and that large firms produce fewer than their public relations image would suggest. Yet the greatest loss probably stems from the vast quantity of socially beneficial research and innovation not now being done at all, especially that not being done at the basic research level. Should the Federal government seriously devote its financial resources to furthering peacetime research, the technical underpinnings for rapid full-employment growth would certainly multiply.

12. *Forbes,* Vol. 98, No. 5 (September 1, 1966), p. 45.

A Parting Thought

THE CONSIDERATIONS stressed by microeconomic theory—efficiency, proper resource allocation—are important, and American industrial performance in efficiency and allocation could unquestionably be improved. But in comparative terms the U.S. microeconomic performance is commendable. Our antitrust strictures, dating back to legislation passed in the late nineteenth century, seem to have preserved us from the worst abuses of monopoly. But the best thing that can happen in an economic system is rapid and sustained economic growth. Even while indulging in a marginal misallocation of shoes and cars, a growing economy that maintains full employment can increase its supply of both shoes and cars. A fully employed economy can outrun its petty misallocations.

The center economy exhibits less price competition than does the periphery; it produces more advertising and monopoly profit. In the absence of strong government support for wage and price guidelines, center firms in investment goods industries may try to boost the price of capital equipment before full employment is reached. Center firms can often set minimum prices, but they cannot be expected to fix price maximums based on productivity gains. This is the government's responsibility. The center economy can have a large influence on the individual's propensity to consume, but it cannot insure adequate purchasing power for all things produced. This is what the government must do. The center economy will provide small product improvements and a few basic innovations. But government must bear the major cost of basic research and perhaps underwrite the initial stages of product development when the technology involved is large-scale and expensive.

The center economy, in conjunction with the Federal government, has a major role to play in the creation of perpetual prosperity. Center firms, especially those firmly embedded in key industries, are semipublic institutions. The recognition of this fact is long overdue. They do not, will not, and cannot adhere to the competitive rules of neoclassical price theory. Traditional competitive theory when applied to center firms is useful pri-

marily in pointing up the price we pay in efficiency for allowing
center firms to structure industrial markets. A professional economic
nomic consensus agrees that the cost is significant in absolute
amount but yet a trivial portion of U.S. national income.

It seems likely that, since about 1961, we have been witness-
ing in America the feeble beginnings of a new economic era
—the creation of a perpetual full-employment economy. Since
World War II, most center firms have developed good, highly
flexible planning mechanisms, many utilizing the new input-
output techniques that Soviet planners find so useful. It is not
true, as some contend, that the American economy is now unplanned. Some of the world's best economic planning takes
place in the United States at the *firm level*. The next step toward perpetual prosperity is the provision of a basis for the coordination of firm plans, particularly in key industries, to assure
a rough equality between *industry capacity* and *industry demand*. Since coordination of private investment plans, sometimes
called collusion, is prohibited by longstanding U.S. antitrust
laws, this necessary management will probably fall to government. The long-run maintenance of full-employment growth
requires a dynamic equilibrium between demand and capacity.
As we learned during the 1930's, a private enterprise economy
may at times provide a rough equality between demand and
capacity without government intervention, but it will not do so
consistently for long periods of time.

During the past few years economics has enjoyed considerable
public prestige. The Council of Economic Advisers has become
a strong voice in the highest councils of government. Few informed laymen would dispute that economists have something
important to say. Yet this enhanced reputation rests heavily on
the doctrines of macroeconomic theory. With the exception of
antitrust, experts in microtheory are seldom queried for advice
on matters of urgent public policy; even in antitrust policy,
lawyers are probably as influential as economists. In this instance
the public and their elected officials judge the profession with
an astonishing clarity of vision. The U.S. economy's most prominent postwar deficiency, and its greatest hope for abundance,
lies in the areas of full employment and growth. On these mat-

ters microtheory says little that has not been said for two generations.

This book might be called a microeconomic supplement to the "new economics" of macro policy. To pursue the goal of perpetual prosperity, we must go beyond a theory of "the firm" and formulate theories of specific types of firms and industries. The division of firms into center and periphery, of industries into key and nonkey, and of production modes into unit and small batch, large batch and mass, and process production is only a beginning. But that beginning must be made; the tools for a microeconomics of full employment and growth are rapidly becoming available. Input-output forecasts *allowing* firms to plan on a national basis are clearly feasible. An outstanding recent example estimates the growth of output, employment, and productivity in ninety U.S. industries.[13] Financed in part by North American Aviation and developed at the Harvard University Research Project on the Structure of the American Economy, these projections are already being put to use by several center firm planners.

There is good reason to believe that center firms, especially the most diversified ones whose interests closely coincide with that of the total economy, will be amenable to basing their decisions on economic projections that *assume* a continuation of full employment. And the assumption by men at the economic center that perpetual prosperity has arrived is an important precondition for its arrival. To the extent that perpetual prosperity paves the way for continuous flow production in cyclically sensitive industries, it will lower production costs.

Perhaps the most important implication of a "new economics of microstructure" is that, given the present organization of American industry, we can attain perpetual prosperity while retaining a high level of what the business community calls "economic freedom." In fact, moral suasion by government is much more effective in highly concentrated industries dominated by center firms than elsewhere.[14] If the number of impor-

---

13. Clopper Almon, Jr., *The American Economy to 1975*, Harper and Row, Publishers, 1966.
14. For a detailed discussion of the relationship between market structure and the effectiveness of moral suasion by government, see J. T. Romans, "Moral Suasion as an Instrument of Economic Policy," *American Economic Review*, Vol. LVI, No. 5 (December, 1966), pp. 1,220–1,225.

tant firms in an industry is small, those violating the "public interest" are easily identified and subjected to public censure. In key industries dominated by a few center firms, necessary controls can remain "voluntary" *and* effective, particularly when employment is less than full.

The managerial and technical strength at the American economic center is greater today than ever before. What is lacking is a network that intermeshes public and private planning into a unified system with full-employment growth as its objective. Center firms have so organized the U.S. economy that it need not falter from atomistic anarchy. They have created a reasonably flexible industrial organization, but they cannot provide the unity of purpose and direction necessary to achieve an efficiently produced, cumulatively growing full-employment abundance. The new structural microeconomics places this responsibility in the same hands that the new macroeconomics shows must handle prosperity through the maintenance of aggregate demand. The American business center will hold, but without government support it will not hold the promise of maximum economic welfare.

Selected Bibliography

NONE OF THESE WRITERS uses the terms "center" or "periphery." Perhaps few of them would agree with my definition of these concepts. Yet all of the listed readings are highly suggestive when viewed in the light of American economic dualism.

American Business

Alfred D. Chandler, Jr., *Strategy and Structure: Chapters in the History of Industrial Enterprise*, M.I.T. Press, 1962. (Also available as an Anchor Books paperback, Doubleday & Company, Inc., 1966.) *The best single source on the rise of the center economy. In addition to chapters on historical background and the spread of the multidivisional corporate structure, Chandler examines four center firms in detail—DuPont, General Motors, Standard Oil (N.J.), and Sears.*

Michael Gort, *Diversification and Integration in American Industry*, Princeton University Press, 1959. *A thorough study of the postwar pattern of large firm diversification and integration.*

John C. Narver, *Conglomerate Mergers and Market Competition*, University of California Press, 1967. *A careful study of the competitive effects of conglomerate mergers and their implications for antitrust.*

U.S. Senate, Committee on the Judiciary, Subcommittee on Antitrust and Monopoly, *Economic Concentration, Part I, Overall and Conglomerate Aspects*, & *Part II, Mergers and Other Factors Affecting*

Industry Concentration, U. S. Government Printing Office, 1964.
An invaluable collection of research findings and individual views pertaining to the center economy in the postwar period. These volumes include expert testimony by M. A. Adelman, Joel Dirlam, Corwin Edwards, Michael Gort, Richard Heflebower, Carl Kaysen, Gardiner Means, Ralph Nelson, William G. Shepherd, and Leonard Weiss.

Foreign Business Dualism

Joe S. Bain, *International Differences in Industrial Structure,* Yale University Press, 1966.
A comparative study of industrial structure in eight major industrial nations during the 1950's.
Seymour Broadbridge, *Industrial Dualism in Japan,* Aldine Publishing Company, 1966.
An examination of the best known case of industrial dualism.

Labor

Otto Eckstein and Thomas A. Wilson, "The Determination of Money Wages in American Industry," *Quarterly Journal of Economics,* Vol. LXXVI, No. 3 (August, 1962).
An examination of the characteristics and extent of pattern bargaining since World War II.
Frank C. Pierson, *Unions in Postwar America,* Random House, Inc., 1967.
An economic assessment of postwar unionism in the center economy (chapter 3), in the periphery economy (chapter 4), and in construction and trucking (chapter 5).

Technical Anatomy of Industry

Joan Woodward, *Industrial Organization: Theory and Practice,* Oxford University Press, 1965.
A superior study of technical production types and their importance to the internal management structure of business firms.

Technology

Daniel Hamberg, *R. & D: Essays on the Economics of Research and Development,* Random House, Inc., 1966.
Considers a variety of economic questions concerning research and development, including the importance of firm size.

Edwin Mansfield, *The Economics of Technological Change*, W. W. Norton & Company, Inc., 1968.
A brief, nonmathematical introduction to the economics of technological change.

Richard R. Nelson, Merton J. Peck, & Edward D. Kalachek, *Technology Economic Growth and Public Policy*, Brookings Institution, 1967.
The authors recommend a Federally financed National Institute of Technology for the promotion of research and development, to be accompanied by an Industrial Extension Service modelled after the Agricultural Extension Service.

Theory of the Firm

Robin Marris, *The Economic Theory of Managerial Capitalism*, The Free Press of Glencoe, 1964.
Building on Mrs. Penrose's work, Marris develops a microeconomics of the center economy.

Edith Penrose, *The Theory of the Growth of the Firm*, Basil Blackwell & Mott, Ltd., 1959.
A pioneer attempt to separate the center and periphery economies. Mrs. Penrose's time perspective is very long run.

Peter J. D. Wiles, *Price Cost and Output* (Revised Edition), Frederick A. Praeger, 1963.
The microeconomic implications of L-shaped cost curves is explored in chapter 12. Wiles also considers the importance of the technical production type to the firm.

Index